Who is Amy (

By

Alan Graham

ISBN: 9781917129619

Original Cover Artwork: Dee Luntley, French Window

For Sheila

Chapters

Thanks

1

It had been one of those weeks when everything had just blown up in my face. Deadlines had already been missed and, worst of all, my final report for the upcoming end of year research meeting hadn't been handed over in time to get printed. And whose fault was that? Mine of course. I simply hadn't managed my time sensibly and now I was about to hit the wall.

My day had begun as it so often does, sitting in my office on the ground floor of the Mathematics faculty building, staring intently at a screen. Out of the corner of my eye I could see Stacey standing in my open office doorway. Stacey was the coolest secretary I'd ever had the pleasure to work with — bright, hard-working and with a great sense of fun. With my eyes still fixed on the screen I managed to say, 'Hi Stace! What's up?'

She laughed. 'You must have sensed my presence?' she replied.

I managed to give her a half smile in return. 'Ever hopeful for your presents, Stacey, but they never seem to come my way!'

'Not entirely true this morning, however!' She nodded at a pile of large reports that she was carrying in both arms. 'Guess what!' she continued. 'Your research project reports have just come through from the print unit!'

'What?!' I replied excitedly. 'I don't believe it!'

I took them from her, set them on a chair and gave her a giant hug.

'But we were sure they weren't going to be finished this week. Thank you so much, Stacey. You must have worked like stink to get this lot reformatted and through the system. You've really got me off the hook!'

Stacey shrugged. 'Don't thank me. It was all down to Amy. She's the one who's been working through her lunch breaks all last week.

'Oh my God!' I replied. 'Thank you, Amy! Hang on …Amy? Who's Amy again?'

'Doh, I can't believe …! In my office, by the window.'

'Ah… yes… dark hair, nice smile.'

'No, that's Janice. Amy is light brown hair and normally very little smile, particularly when you walk into the room.'

'Well, I can't have done anything to upset her … can I?'

Stacey smiled and shook her head. 'Amy's shy—very shy.'

'Oh dear. Well, I'm afraid I haven't really noticed her.'

'Oh God, you're hopeless! Although, reading between the lines, I'd say she's noticed you.'

I gave her a quick glance. 'Oh, come on Stacey!'

'I think you need to pop over and say thanks. In fact, you could buy her a drink, why don't you? She deserves it!'

'Really? I don't think I need to go that far…!'

'Yes, you do! It won't kill you, will it?'

'Well, I'll think about it, Stacey.'

Stacey made a face. 'By the way, you're not in tomorrow, are you?'

'I'll be out all morning.'

'OK, see you later!'

She disappeared down the corridor and for a moment I just sat there trying to picture who this Amy was.

The next day was Wednesday, a day when I was involved in a full morning visit to a local primary school where I'd planned to run a series of workshops with a class of Year 5 children. I arrived just as the children had returned to their various classrooms from school assembly. After signing myself in to the school office, I collected my visitor's ID badge and pinned it to my jacket. At that moment I bumped into Mrs Ahmed, the head teacher.

'Here again Mr Campbell! You just can't stay away, can you!'

I shook her hand. 'Hi Mrs Ahmed. No, you're right. This has definitely become my happy place!'

Mrs Ahmed smiled. 'So, what do you and Kathy have planned for today?'

'Oh, the usual. We've prepared pages and pages of very hard sums!'

She laughed this time. 'Well, I seriously doubt that! But whatever you do with them, I know they'll just love it. The children are very excited that you're coming. I'll walk you round.'

As we walked along the corridor to Kathy's classroom, I outlined briefly what activities we had planned for the forthcoming lesson on the themes of chance and coincidences. She listened intently as I talked and then said 'Well, the hard sums will have to wait. Who knew that maths could be so much fun?'

She tapped on Kathy's classroom door and all eyes turned to their smiling head teacher. 'Miss Brooke, Class 5, your visitor has arrived. Do come in, Mr Campbell.' To my surprise and delight, this introduction inspired a mini cheer from the children. I smiled at Kathy and stepped in front of the class. 'OK, Year 5. Who's very excited about spending the whole morning doing lots of lovely maths?'

A few of the children managed a rather lukewarm response of 'We are!' I shook my head in faux disappointment. 'No, no, that won't do at all!'

I cupped my hand over my ear and said again much louder. 'OK then. Who's very excited about spending the whole morning doing lots of lovely maths?' This time the whole class joined in and the chorus of 'We are!' was deafening. The head teacher laughed as she waved us all goodbye and walked out of the door.

'So, Year 5, let's start with a question. Does anybody here think that they are lucky?' Most of the children put their hands up. 'So why do you think that?' I continued. Then Seth called out, 'We're lucky you're here today sir because now we won't have to do any hard sums!' We all had a good laugh at that one.

3

'OK, see what you make of this. A famous tennis player once said that the harder she works the luckier she seems to get. What do you think she meant by that?'

And so began a very lively class discussion about luck, chance and coincidence.

The following morning began with my usual visit to Stacey's office. I glanced over to the window on the left of the room. 'Hi Amy!' I gave her the best smile I could muster. She glanced back with an uncertain gaze and then looked down.

'Hi,' she replied, sounding like she was the only kid at the party who'd come in fancy dress.

'Thanks so much for doing that report. You really got me out of a jam.'

Amy reddened and continued to look at the carpet.

I returned to my office. At least I'd managed to tick the box marked, "Say thanks". She did indeed look shy. Quite an interesting face, though. I looked again at the pile of research reports that apparently Amy had done for me. It really was a massive job. At lunchtime, while all the secretaries were on the field eating their lunch, I left a note on her desk.

Hi Amy, I'm popping over to the Campus Bar at 5.30-ish for a quick one. Can I buy you a drink to say thank you?'
Pete

That afternoon was spent bashing the computer, trying to finish off a spreadsheet that should have been done and dusted the previous week. As 5.30 approached, people started walking down the corridor. Then I heard a rustling and a hint of a *sotto voce* cough. I looked up to see Amy.

'Hi, Amy! Good to see you!'

She shook her head. 'I can't … sorry.'

'Oh, that's a pity. Never mind …'

'My dad…' Her voice trailed off.

I gave her an encouraging smile and waited.

'… picking me up at a quarter to…'

'Ah well, erm, Amy. It was just an idea.'

She turned to go and I really thought that was that. Then she turned back and said quietly, 'Monday, maybe?'

'Great!' I said with as much enthusiasm as I could muster. 'Monday it is. Same time, same place!'

'OK,' she replied. 'So, 5.30 and ... shall I come here?'

'Yes, that's fine.'

She turned and disappeared.

I sat back in my chair and thought 'Seriously, Stacey! What have you got me into here?' Amy looked very young but was probably in her early twenties. I was 36. I couldn't imagine what we had in common, other than work. What on Earth were we going to talk about on Monday? I wonder if she likes Ella Fitzgerald? Has she even heard of Ella Fitzgerald?

Did I find her attractive? Not sure. How do people judge these things, anyway? She definitely wasn't glamorous. She seemed to be more of a jumper-and-jeans sort of a girl—a simple bobbed hairstyle and not much in the way of make-up. Weighing it all up, I'd say more "looking good" than "good-looking". But she did seem nice.

2

I spent the following weekend at a maths teaching conference held at Reading University. I'd been invited to give a talk on pupil perceptions of chance and luck, with the catchy title "What are the Chances of that Happening?" The event was quite well attended and seemed to be enjoyed— although I suspect most of my audience were escapees from the alternative talks on offer which may have looked a lot less fun.

I started by asking the participants to play a game that I call "washing line". A piece of string was strung across the room with the words *impossible* at one end and *certain* at the other. Then I invited them to come up with as many words or phrases as they could think of that described degrees of likelihood ('possible', 'probable', 'rare' 'a long shot' and so on) and each word or phrase was written on a card. The game is to try to peg the cards onto the washing line in their appropriate positions between the two extremes. And if any of the words is preceded by 'very' or 'fairly' or 'not', where does that send it to along the washing line?

Afterwards we moved on to talking about the so-called Gambler's Fallacy. This misconception leads punters to believe that, after a string of losses, their next bet is more likely to win. Oh dear!

We ended the session with a 400-year journey back in time to enter the mind of French philosopher, Blaise Pascal. Here is one of his more intriguing ideas:

Le cœur a ses raisons que la raison ne connaît point.

This translates as:

The heart has its reasons which reason knows nothing of.

In other words, we know the truth not only by our powers of reasoning, but also by what we feel in our heart. Pascal suggests here that the heart may, perhaps even subconsciously, provide us with insights that the mind has no access to. But, crucially, can we really grasp exactly what it is that the heart is feeling?

The teachers agreed that many of their pupils could be interested in these sorts of questions but we had to acknowledge that they were not issues that are much explored in classroom lessons on probability. Most of the time, students are expected to remove themselves from their personal intuitions and focus exclusively on the information provided in the textbook question.

Overall, I had a good time at Reading and was able to meet up with quite a few colleagues whom I hadn't seen for ages. Just to have a chat and a drink with old friends was a welcome diversion. These days, now that I was increasingly and, probably irrevocably, on my own, I tended to fill my weekends with work-related activities. Over the previous few months, I'd been living quite close to the university in a small, rented flat. But in truth, I hadn't really cracked the social scene of Milton Keynes. I was friendly with a few workmates/colleagues but they were mostly married, had kids and were living elsewhere—too busy and too unavailable to provide me with any real companionship. So, in my free time I mostly just kept myself to myself, strumming my guitar, listening to music, attending the odd concert or catching a theatre play in the local playhouse, almost always on my own. I was also using the space to write up my thesis and get that doctorate albatross off my back. This was the one bit of good news in my life as I really felt that good progress on the write-up was being made at last.

Monday quickly came around and I surprisingly found myself rather looking forward to my drink with the mysterious but shy Amy. As usual, I kicked the day off with a quick trip to Stacey's office. I checked out the desk by the window but it was empty. 'No Amy today?' I asked Stacey.

'Not yet,' she replied. 'Apparently, she's having transport problems. We might see her later this morning.'

'What's the problem? Dad's car broken down?'

Stacey nodded. 'Yea, they're stuck on the Marina roundabout waiting for the RAC. I think she's got herself into a bit of a state about it all.'

'Oh, that's a shame!'

I turned to exit the door.

'Hey Pete. Do you have your car today?'

I nodded.

'You'd be there in five. Pop over and get her would you?'

'Really? I've such a lot on though, Stacey, …'

'Pete,' Stacey said, with her serious face on. 'She's upset! Just do a nice thing for her!'

I shrugged. 'OK, mamma Stacey. I'll do it! Can you give her a buzz and tell her I'll be there in 5 minutes?'

Stacey shook her head. 'Not so easy. Her phone's packed in!'

'You're kidding! So how did you know she'd broken down?'

'They give this other girl a lift and Amy phoned me with *her* phone.'

I pondered this for a moment. 'So, what car does her dad drive, then?'

'It's a van, I think. And green. Hmm … or is it? Well, let's say greenish.'

'Thanks Stacey. Don't overload me with any more forensic detail! That's probably all I need. I'd better be off!'

Five minutes later I was approaching the Marina roundabout. Parked up on the inside lane was an RAC Rescue vehicle and right next to it, a small dark blue van. Amy and her friend were standing on the roundabout while a very red-faced dad seemed to be having some sort of argy-bargy with the repair man. I pulled in as close as I could get to the roundabout and waved to Amy. At first, she looked startled and then waved back. She shouted something to her dad, who was still in full flow and didn't seem to notice. Then Amy and her friend ran to my car and stopped at my open window.

'Special university rescue service …' I began.

Amy's friend jumped into the passenger seat while Amy climbed into the back.

'… Hi, I'm Marcie,' said my front seat passenger. 'I'm in the Payroll department. What's your name, by the way?'

'Pete.'

'Pete, well thanks ever so much Pete, you've really saved my bacon. I suppose you work with Amy. Funny she's never mentioned you … Anyway, you've no idea … you see, we've got a big payroll transition going on this week and they totally need me to be there …'

And so Marcie continued without drawing breath for the full five minutes of the journey. Through the rear-view mirror, I glanced at Amy sitting in silence behind me. She wore no expression that I could discern. When we got to the university car park, Marcie thanked me again and unbuckled her seat belt. Then, to my surprise, she leant across and kissed me on the cheek. 'My hero!' she whispered and scampered off to save the entire university payroll from imminent disaster.

I smiled at Amy through the mirror. She lightly touched my shoulder and said quietly, 'Thank you so much!'

I looked at her more closely and thought I could discern just a hint of a smile there—but I couldn't be sure. Then she said nervously, 'I'm so late, what will Stacey think of me?'

Then she too ran off to where she was needed. All that remained of the interaction was the faintest, lingering hint of her perfume where her hand had brushed my jumper.

Later that morning I received a call from a couple of academic colleagues from New Zealand who were over on a sabbatical visit. They had attended my weekend session at Reading and wanted to take the probability ideas further. They'd popped by to explore an interesting idea for a joint UK/NZ project involving pupil expectations and assumptions about chance, by creating an application called "Game of Chance". It all looked interesting and I was keen to find out more about it.

Before I knew it, it was 5.25pm. I had only just started to move a few things from my desk and into my briefcase when my office phone rang. Who could this be, I wondered?

It was an unfamiliar female voice with a slight French accent.

' 'ello, Mr 'ero …'

'No … my name is Campbell, Peter Campbell …'

'Sorry to bother you Mr 'ero but you're to have a visitor shortly. Someone called Marcie from the Payroll department. She'll be here in a few minutes…'

'No, no, I can't see her,' I stammered. 'I have a VERY important meeting at 5.30. Just put her off, can you.'

'Oh? OK, Mr 'ero. I'll see what I can do.'

She rang off.

Thirty seconds later there was a figure standing at the door. 'Bonjour! Mr 'ero.' Amy looked at me and actually smiled. Yes, she actually smiled!

Wow! Who could have seen that coming? Shy, silent Amy had played me like a fiddle!

Drinks

3

We walked together to the campus bar. Nothing was said but it seemed to me like an easy silence that we both found comfortable. I opened the main door and stepped aside to let her go in first. Amy stood on the threshold looking apprehensive and shook her head.

'No please, after you,' she responded.

I tried to do as she requested and attempted that tricky manoeuvre of walking through the door while still trying to hold it open for her. Awkward or what, but we managed it in the end!

The bar was fairly empty and we were able to find a corner seat by the window. I smiled at Amy. 'I'm going to need a drink after that stunt you pulled! I'm getting myself a bottle of Bud.' Amy lowered her head. 'So, what can I get you then?' I asked. Amy frowned. 'Oh, erm, nothing special. Really, it's a bit too early for me for a ...for a proper drink... I might just have a ...' After a rather long silence, I decided to jump in.

'How about a cheeky apple juice or maybe you could risk a Fever Tree tonic water?'

She nodded. 'One of those would be ...'

I sat holding a bottle of Budweiser while Amy downed her fruit juice in one. 'Blimey!' I remarked. 'It must be thirsty work dealing in fraud and subterfuge!'

We looked at each other for a moment, both unsure where to start.

'Well, here we are,' I began. 'Actually, the first time we've ever had a proper conversation, eyeball to eyeball...'

Amy looked startled. She started to speak but put her hand over her mouth. She whispered 'Sorry ... I can't ...' Then she stood up as if to leave.

11

I looked at her, concerned. 'Are you going to be sick?'

She shook her head. 'It's, it's just that … I'm hopeless in these …'

Amy looked like a lost kitten.

I took her hand and gently encouraged her to sit back on her chair.

'Please don't leave, Amy.'

I suddenly felt really sad for her. Perhaps a change of tack was required. So … my golden rule is, when in doubt, talk about your mother.

'You know what my mother always used to tell me?' I began. 'She said the best conversation you have with a person isn't at a party or where you're sitting looking at each other face-to-face. It's when you're doing a practical job together—like gardening or washing the dishes. That's when conversation just seems to flow naturally.'

Amy nodded slowly. 'Wise woman,' she said. I waited for more but nothing was forthcoming.

'Anyway,' I went on, 'I can't let this inaugural meeting continue without giving you some important information.'

She raised her eyebrows.

'First of all, can you tell me, why did the, urm, chicken cross the playground?'

Amy stared blankly.

'I'm going to have to tell you then!'

She nodded weakly with her eyes.

'To get to the other *slide*!'

'Ah,' she replied, still unsmiling. 'Slide. I see.'

I continued. 'There's another important slide-related question that I'd like to put to you.'

'OK,' she replied slowly.

'What did the dog say while sitting on a sandpaper slide?'

A gentle shake of the head from Amy.

'Ruff!'

At last, a discernible hint of a smile this time.

'Just one more and then I'll stop. What do you call a Frenchman wearing sandals?'

Amy narrowed her eyes. 'I know it! Phillipe … Phillope?', she replied, carefully.

I clapped my hands. 'Well done! You're getting the hang of this.'

Then Amy said 'Where did you find those terrible jokes? I don't even know how you can remember them.'

'Well,' I replied, 'I'm creating a website for my two nephews. It's called *ChuckleBoys*. We do two new jokes every week and these are the latest in a long line of rib-ticklers.'

Amy settled back into her chair and was visibly starting to relax. 'Tell me about them, these boys,' she asked.

'OK. Their mum's my sister, she's Annie. The boys are called Harry and Sam.'

'Ages?'

'Oh, Harry's 9 and Sam is 7. I think you'd like them.'

Amy nodded slowly and then looked away, 'Harry and Sam. I bet I would.' She paused. 'I suppose they think you're some sort of 'ero!' She pronounced the word in the French manner, giving the 'r' an extended detour around the back of her tonsils.

'Something like that!' I smiled back.

Crisis averted. By now Amy had returned to planet Earth and seemed unlikely to want to head for the hills any time soon.

'Now, don't go anywhere,' I said sternly. 'I'm going to get you another one. How about a *proper drink* this time?'

'Oh,' said Amy, looking confused. Then she pointed at my bottle of Budweiser. 'I think I might just have…a bottle of Bud.' The bar was still almost empty of customers so I quickly got her one.

'Did you know,' I said when I returned, 'that Amy is an anagram of May?'

'And also of Yam!' she replied.

'Hmm, but there is no known anagram for my name,' I continued confidently.

She considered this proposition for a moment.

'Apart from TePe—you know those little interdental brushes—that's an anagram for Pete. And Peter, let me see. Well, if you're allowed to use French, *répét* is the root of *répéter*, to repeat.'

I was suddenly slightly stunned. Where did shy, nervous Amy go? Who is this person? Suddenly I felt she was sufficiently relaxed to have a real conversation.

'Wow! How come your French is so good?'

'Ah, that's a long story,' she replied, blushing a little.

'OK then. Can I ask you another question? You know that phone call you made to me— Monsieur 'ero and all that.'

Amy nodded.

'Well, that was pretty funny! But how come you can pull a number like that and then … sort of want to take flight when we first sat down here?'

Amy looked nervous and thoughtful. Eventually she started to speak. 'I seem to be fine on the phone. But when I'm in the same room with people and them staring at me, well I sometimes just go to pieces. I seem to lose the power of speech. It's so embarrassing— I just want the ground to swallow me up. I'd rather not … you know… '

I suddenly felt responsible. 'Was this incident something I did … or said?'

'Oh, it's not your fault. But it doesn't take much. I think it was that expression you used, "eyeball-to-eyeball". That just … set me off.'

I put a hand on her shoulder, 'Sorry Amy, I had no idea…'

'No, it's not you. It's just something I have to … you know …'

After a few moments' silence, I returned to more practical matters. 'How's your dad's van doing? Will it be back on the road any time soon?'

She shook her head. 'Not sure. It'll be out of action for a while, I think.'

'So how are you getting home tonight?'

Suddenly in bounced Marcie who sat down in one of the empty chairs.

'By bus!' she interrupted. 'I've sorted it all out and there's one at the gatehouse in about fifteen minutes.'

'Oh, right then!' Amy began to gather her bits together and stood up to go.

'Oh, Amy,' I interjected. 'Just before you go, you said you were going to tell Marcie one of those jokes you were telling me. Tell her that French one.'

Amy made an intense how-could-you-do-this-to-me face. Then she took a very deep breath. 'OK then.'

She turned to face Marcie. 'Marcie, What do you call a Frenchman wearing sandals?'

Marcie looked at Amy in amazement. 'I, I don't think I erm ...', she trailed off.

'Phillipe Phillope ... naturallement!' This time Amy gave full rein to what sounded to me to be an excellent French accent, all accompanied by a classic Gallic shrug.

Marcie's face looked blank. Then she gave me a conspiratorial look as if we shared the secret of Amy's descent into madness. 'If you say so, Amy. Now let's go. We'd better get a wiggle on.'

Then I added, 'Can I just check, Amy. I think we have another important meeting next week. It's same time, same place.'

After a moment's hesitation Amy cottoned on. 'Ah yes,' she replied. 'It's already in my diary.'

Bye, then, bye ... bye.'

I watched as the two young women made their way to the exit. Marcie was in full conversational flow. Then, at the door, Amy suddenly stopped, turned and looked at me. In a single gesture she smiled, shrugged her shoulders, raised her eyebrows and flashed her eyes. It was all over in less than half a second but it simply took my breath away. Instinctively, I waved back and then ... she was gone.

I stood up to finish my drink and with the other hand picked up Amy's bottle to return them both to the bar. Only then did I notice that hers was still full. I was sure I'd seen her raise it to her mouth periodically during our conversation but none of the contents seemed to have got past her lips. I sat down again, put her bottle to my own lips and began to complete the task myself.

15

'So, new bird, then. Isn't she a bit young for you, Mr Campbell?' It was Simon from the Statistics department who clapped me on the shoulder and sat down on the stool that Amy had just vacated.

'Oh no, not at all,' I laughed. 'Just a colleague.'

Simon laughed. 'Oh yea! If you say so. My lips are sealed. Hey, are you still good for the five-aside game tomorrow. It's against IT so that's going to be a right needle match.'

I smiled back. 'I'll be there, don't worry. They walloped us last time so there are a few scores to settle I'd say!'

'Can I buy you a pint?' Simon asked.

'No, I've still got one here,' I replied pointing to the bottle in my hand. 'I'll bring it over and join you at the bar.'

4

I drove straight home, reheated and rapidly demolished the remains of a fish pie that I'd made two days before. As had been my nightly routine for many months, I sat down at my desk and opened up the file on my computer marked Pete's Thesis. I was determined to tear into the chapter that had been giving me grief for some time— *Chance and Intuition.* This was a theme that was central to my thesis topic so it was pretty important to be able to present these ideas in a form that supported the story I wanted to tell. I had done much research and reading on this particular theme but the problem was that, when it all boiled down, I really wasn't sure what my central point was to be. Yes, there were lots of examples where people's faulty intuitions about chance events compromised their ability to make good life decisions. But it was also possible that their intuitions captured something important about how they *really* saw the world and which wasn't ever properly acknowledged when the logical part of the brain was in charge. These two ideas seemed to pull in opposite directions.

I thought back to the attendees at the weekend conference and remembered how interested they had been in the ideas of Blaise Pascal. I hoped that for most of them, the take-away message was how students' personal intuitions are too often seen as irrelevant to their learning. In fact, in most mathematics classrooms, the emotions associated with these personal feelings are designated as strictly no-go areas. So called "real life problems" are usually nothing of the kind as they are invariably set within rigid and impossibly simplistic contexts.

My mind kept returning to the corner table of the campus bar and that half-second frisson of intense emotion that I experienced when

Amy waved goodbye. Catching her smile and sharing a brief moment of direct eye contact with her had felt like the rarest of gifts. Suddenly what Pascal had been writing about almost 400 years earlier started to have some resonance for my own intuitions when it came to making close relationships. All logic said that a relationship with Amy didn't make sense, yet here was my heart strongly sending me a very different message.

I barely knew this young woman and yet I couldn't stop thinking about her. One thing I was sure about— I wanted to see her again and definitely before the following Monday. But did she feel the same? Well, if Blaise Pascal was right and *the heart knows what the mind knows not of*, I needed to start trusting my own intuitions. I knew that I'd never know the answer for certain until I made contact with Amy again. Perhaps I should ask to see her at lunchtime the following day, or would that be too pushy?

What would my mother advise? Ah, yes! She always used to say, "Faint heart ne'er won fair maid". Thanks, mum. I opened up my email, selected Amy's name and typed:

'Amy, Lunch tomorrow? Pete x'

I hovered the mouse over the SEND button, closed my eyes and clicked it with my eyes still closed. Thirty seconds later, she replied.

'Pete, ☺ ☺, A x'

Crumbs, you've done it, Pete. No turning back now!

Although not wanting to admit it, I'd been increasingly isolated since Clare set off for her new job in California twelve months previously. Of course, we'd agreed to stay in regular contact but gradually over the months the phone calls had become shorter and the emails less frequent. It came as a jolt to realise that it was fully two months since I'd actually had any contact with Clare at all. Weirdly, after having been together for 12 years, I wasn't grieving for her or missing her company. It was just that I was finding life ... a bit lonely.

At 12.30 the following day, Amy and I were seated opposite each other at a little table in the refectory. She smiled.

'Eyeball to eyeball again, eh?' I grinned.

Amy kept smiling this time. 'Not such a problem today,' she replied.

'So, we're friends now?' I asked.

'If you say so,' she responded. 'But can I ask you a question?'

I nodded.

'Why are you interested in me?'

'Why wouldn't I be? I like ... the cut of your jib.'

'My jib?' Amy looked confused. 'But ... boys have never been particularly interested in me. Here I am at 23, and ...' she hesitated. I could see her eyes start to well up. She got a tissue out of her bag and blew her nose.

'Well,' she continued, 'I know I'm not what you'd call ... very attractive.'

I frowned. 'Says who?'

'I just know that's what people think.'

I raised my eyebrows. 'I need names. Tell me who said that and they'll get a punch in the mouth!'

Amy laughed at this proposition.

'Well,' she went on, 'my bottom's too big for a start. My dad sometimes calls me ...' Amy stopped, suddenly looking embarrassed.

'He calls you...?' I probed.

'He calls me ...lardy!'

I was appalled. 'He what?! Your bottom is *perfect*. Look,' I continued, 'you won't know this but it's the talk of the faculty how perfect it is.'

Amy's eyes widened.

Oh dear—perhaps I'd gone too far here. Anyway, I decided to keep digging and hope to come out the other side in one piece.

'As a matter of fact, it just came up at last week's faculty board meeting.'

Amy raised an eyebrow as she looked at me in disbelief.

'Yes,' I continued. 'We had an advertising executive in to give us an *inspirational* talk about how we could encourage more students to take our higher-level courses. He explained that these specialist courses lacked everyday appeal and, *going forward,* we needed to start "selling the sizzle, not the sausage"; in other words, we needed to find some perfect metaphor for why these harder courses were cool. Everyone in the room nodded. Then the Dean said, "I'll tell you what's bloody perfect. If you're looking for a great metaphor then look no further than that secretary Amy's bottom." Everyone in the room nodded again.'

Fortunately, I could see that the more my tale was growing ever more outlandish, the more relaxed Amy's expression was becoming.

'The dean! My! So, what happened then?' she gasped.

'Oh, our guest said he didn't know Amy and it was probably a great, urm, metaphor but overall, he felt that this mightn't be the most progressive erm, motif for our faculty's image, going forward.'

By now Amy was rocking in her chair with laughter. She shook her head and mouthed, 'I don't think so.'

'In the end we went for another metaphor.'

'Which was?' Amy managed to ask.

'We came back to the sausage,' I replied. 'Sure, everybody loves a sausage!'

After Amy had wiped away tears of laughter, we both sat quietly for a moment. She looked away, occupied by her own thoughts. Then she said slowly, 'Just to be clear, Pete, none of this is true, of course. This Faculty Board stuff. It really is all a creation of your … febrile imagination.'

I smiled at her. 'I promise. It's all bollocks! Apart from that sausage thing, of course — that'll probably happen! No, no, I'm kidding, that's not true either! The faculty isn't even ready for the sausage metaphor just yet.'

'Good,' replied Amy, still smiling but with a trace of relief on her face.

'The point is …' I went on. 'The point of my story is to say … there's nothing even slightly sub-standard about your bottom. I find it attractive and indeed, I find you attractive!'

Amy blushed and looked away. Then she turned back to look at me and said softly 'Thank you. Thank you for saying that.'

I smiled back at her. 'But another thing,' I continued. 'What your dad said, it's just not on. He's going to have to shape up … or else…'

'Or else what...?'

'Or else there'll be a Sandy Row uppercut coming his way sometime soon.'

'Cripes,' spluttered Amy, 'what's one of those?'

'Not entirely sure but he'd better bet he doesn't want one!'

By 2PM we were both back in our offices. I clicked open my email and sent her a message:

Looking forward to our next important meeting. So many questions. Hope to get to the bottom of some of them. P xx

She came straight back with:

'⬛⬛, A xx'

5

Can I ask you a personal question?' Amy asked over a coffee in the refectory a couple of days later.

'Fire away!' I replied. 'My life is an open book!'

Then Amy looked serious. 'Look, we like each other…'

I nodded.

'… and over the past few days we've spent a fair bit of time together, and all that.'

I nodded again.

'Well, that's all great. But, I can't help wondering …Well, I can't believe that a witty, intelligent, sympathetic… erm … help me out here …!'

I jumped in 'er … charismatic, heroic, captivating, mesmerising, …'

'All right, all right,' Amy interrupted. 'Don't go over the top! I'm just asking why a nice guy like you doesn't already have a girlfriend!'

This was an important question that deserved a proper answer. I paused for a few moments before responding. 'Well, I've been with someone called Clare for over ten years now. She's American. She went back to work in California about a year ago and we haven't seen each other since.'

'So,' said Amy slowly, 'Is it … over?'

'Not officially. We still exchange occasional emails—quite friendly and all that but there's no sense of either of us wanting to meet up any time soon.'

Amy considered what I'd just said.

'And is that how you're going to leave it then?'

I patted her hand. 'No. I've been thinking about that and I'm going to tell her.'

Amy's eyes widened. 'Tell her what?'

'Tell her … that I've moved on.'

'Oh,' said Amy. She remained silent for a long time.

Then she said 'So, what exactly are you saying?'

'I'm saying … that I prefer to spend my time with you than with Clare. In fact, I prefer to spend my time with you than with anyone else.'

'Oh!' Amy looked away. 'Well, that's … that's very nice!'

She sat quietly for a few moments. 'And have you been to America … with …Clare?' Amy asked.

'Yes, a couple of times. I've met her folks and one or two of her old school friends. It was quite pleasant, I guess. What about you, Amy? Have you travelled much?'

She considered the question. 'Oh well, you know, the usual. We went to Italy one year … and two years ago we went skiing in the Alps. I just loved skiing—I can't wait to try it again!'

'Was that just you and your dad, then?'

'Yea, that's right. It was really…lovely.'

Then she changed gear. 'OK, another question. Do you like music and, if so, what sort of music do you listen to?'

'Mmm!' I considered the matter carefully. 'Good question! I actually love music. I listen to it a lot—most evenings—and I even play a bit myself.'

She raised her eyebrows.

'Contra-bassoon and glockenspiel, in case you're wondering!'

'Snap!' she replied, cheerfully.

'Well,' she went on. 'Here's an idea. My streaming platform lists my 25 most regularly played tracks. I bet yours does too.'

I nodded.

'OK then. Let's turn these into playlists and swap them. That way we can get to know each other's musical tastes a bit better.'

'I love that idea,' I replied enthusiastically. 'I'll do mine tonight!'

23

'Me too,' said Amy. Then she grinned. 'It's so comforting to think that by tomorrow you'll be singing along to the complete sound track of *Frozen*!'

'Can't wait!' I responded.

'Now, my turn,' I countered. 'I've got a musical question for you. When was the last time you went to a music concert?'

'A concert? Let me see?' Amy said slowly. 'Mmm, it's been months. Oh yes, it was last year in Birmingham.'

'Oh,' I asked. 'Who did you go and see?'

'Well, I can't really remember. A friend took me along. It was a favourite band of hers. I didn't think too much of them, to be honest.'

'Was that at the Symphony Hall... or was it the NEC?'

'Oh, the NEC. But why are you asking?'

'Well, the point is, Miss Carpenter...you're being asked out on a date!'

'Seriously?'

'Indeed. There's a band that I really like and they're playing at The Stables in Wavendon tomorrow night. If I can get tickets, will you come with me?'

Amy clapped her hands. 'Yippee! Amy Carpenter says yes please! I don't care what sort of music they play. I'll just love it. Thank you so much!'

I picked up my phone and checked ticket availability. Success! We were on for the following evening. 'It starts at 8 so shall I pick you up from your place at, let's say, 7.30.'

Amy nodded. 'Tell you what, there's a Greggs just round the corner from where we live. I'll want to buy a couple of things first. Can you meet me there?'

'OK, see you at 7.30 then!'

As arranged, I picked Amy up from the corner shop the following evening. We made our way to The Stables Theatre, both greatly looking forward to enjoying the sweet sounds of The Canny Band. We were directed to the smaller of the two venues which was just perfect for the intimate music of this lively Scottish three-piece folk band. I'd spotted that contemporary Celtic folk music had not been one of the musical genres that had featured in Amy's Top 25 playlist but I knew I was on a winner. In the event, neither of us were disappointed.

Amy was just buzzing with it all as we drove back to my flat for a nightcap. What a transformation since the first time we sat down in the Campus Bar, "eyeball to eyeball". She was still talking about the concert and the music as she entered my flat. It was the first time she had ever crossed the threshold. We sat together side by side on the sofa.

'Amy,' I said, 'As I'm driving, I'm going to have a very small dry white wine. Can I interest you …?'

Amy shook her head. 'Not tonight thanks. Just a glass of water is fine.'

We sat together on the sofa. I took Amy's hand in mine and slid my other arm around her shoulder. 'I thought I might kiss you? What do you think?'

I gently pulled her towards me but was slightly surprised to be met with firm resistance.

'Don't you want to?' I asked.

Amy's eyes started to well up. 'Yes,' she replied. 'Yes, I do want to … but … I can't!'

'Why not?'

For a while, Amy was unable to speak. Then she said 'Do you remember our first meeting when I nearly walked out?'

'How could I forget!' I smiled.

'Well, I'm getting the same now. I'd like to kiss you but … well, my body won't let me. I'm so sorry Pete. We've had such a lovely evening and … I really feel I've spoilt it for both of us.'

'No you haven't, Amy. Yes it has been a lovely evening but this hasn't spoilt anything.'

I paused and held one hand dramatically to my ear.

'Oh, hang on, I've just had a subliminal message from my mum and she's saying … sorry mum, what's that again … oh yes, she says … a message for Amy … tell her that …good things don't always come easy! Thanks mum!'

25

Amy clapped her hands to her face as a mask to hide the emotions that had suddenly filled her heart. Eventually she was able to take her hands away and speak.

'Your mum! She always seems to be able to say just the right thing. What would she make of me, I wonder?'

I gave Amy a measured look. 'She'd just love you to bits. And she'd be looking at me and saying, Peter, you're so lucky to have found that girl. You look after her and make sure you never let her go!'

A tear started running down Amy's cheek. 'Wow,' she said thoughtfully. 'How ...beautiful. But I just hope this ... stupid thing doesn't spoil it all.'

'We won't let it. Look, the two of us together are a team ... we got over that first hurdle in the Campus Bar and we'll get over this one!'

'How?' Amy asked with a worried expression.

'Never fear, for I have a plan!'

Amy started to brighten up a little. 'What plan?'

'Well,' I asked, 'do you like dancing?'

'Never done it!'

'Thought not! Well, I think it's time you did!'

I reached over to pick up my car keys. 'Now, let's get you home!'

Amy stood up to put on her jacket. She turned back to face me. 'Hey, Pete. Thanks!'

'Thanks for what?'

'Oh ... you know!'

6

The following Monday at just 12.40, Amy and I were seated at my dining room table. Amy had just an hour for her lunch break so we were on a pretty tight schedule. As agreed, we had both brought our sandwiches to the dancing class and we quickly consumed them. We dragged the chairs and sofa to the edge of the room to make space. Amy pulled her laptop from her tote bag and quickly found a YouTube video entitled *It takes two to Salsa, Lesson 1*. She fired up Bluetooth and in a few seconds it was streaming on my TV set.

Thirty minutes later we flopped down on the sofa in a heap of exhaustion. 'I loved that, Pete!' Amy panted. 'Thanks so much for thinking up the idea!'

'Yes,' I replied. 'I loved it too. Can't wait for Lesson Two tomorrow.'

'For thinking it up, though…you deserve some sort of reward, surely!' she said, shyly. Amy threw her arms around my neck and planted a big sloppy, sweaty kiss on each cheek.

'Oh!' I gasped in mock surprise. 'Who'd have thought that an innocent little Cuban gyration could lead to this, Miss Carpenter!'

And so it continued through the week as each day we shared a new and ever more energetic Salsa lesson. By Thursday, we both agreed that great progress had been made on the Salsa front. Friday lunchtime came around and as we had done all week, we shared a quick sandwich and then I announced, 'Right, let's get these chairs moving. I feel Lesson 5 coming on!'

Suddenly Amy took my hand. 'Actually, Pete,' she said softly. 'Do you mind if we don't. I'd just like to talk today.'

I smiled. 'Talk, is it? Well, you've come to the right man. What's on your mind?'

'You know this dancing thing we've been doing all week.'

'I certainly do,' I replied.

'Well, you may be amazed to learn that it's not just made me a better dancer, but …'

'…but something else?'

Amy laughed, '…but, as you perfectly well know…because this was why you introduced the idea of salsa in the first place…the experience has had a very positive effect on my phobia about touching!'

'Really?' I asked in mock surprise. 'Well, that's a good thing, then. A very lucky side effect! Tell me, have you always had this problem…with touching?

She considered the question carefully. 'I think so. For as long as I remember. There's no touching with my dad and I don't remember my mum so I've missed out on that from her too. To be honest, until this past few weeks there's never been anyone I've trusted enough to want to get physically close to.'

'That's a real shame, Aims,' I replied. 'Do you think you might have had a bad experience with touching at some point in your life?'

'Yes, a couple of times in my teenage years. I've had boys drunk and over-handsy trying to grab me. I just wasn't prepared for that. It frightened me so much that…well, I ran away and hid. Being very shy was my best protection!'

I stared into her eyes. 'Well, Amy. I'm really sorry.'

We sat quietly for a few moments. Suddenly she said, 'Pete. Could you do me a favour?'

'Of course.'

'Could you just close your eyes and then lick your lips.'

I did as instructed.

She took both of my hands in hers and gave me a long hard kiss on the mouth. Eventually I opened my eyes again.

'Blimey! I didn't see that coming!' was all I could manage to say.

'Of course you didn't,' snorted Amy. 'You had your eyes closed!'

28

We both found this remark surprisingly amusing and started to laugh uproariously.

'So, tell me Pete. How can I become a good kisser?'

'Practice, Miss Carpenter.' I replied. 'It's all down to practice— preferably with the right support worker, of course!'

Amy laughed and kissed me again.

'Hey Aims, there's one thing that we need to talk about.'

Suddenly there was a worried look on her face.

'You're not going to dump me are you? Not now that I've just discovered the joy of kissing.'

I shook my head and smiled back at her. 'Of course not! That thought couldn't be further from my mind. Scout's honour! No, the only cloud that is on our horizon is that … as you know, I'll shortly be going off to teach at summer school for a whole week in distant Stirling….'

Amy made a sad face and acted out the falling of tears from her eyes. 'I'm trying not to think about that. I'm really going to miss you, Pete!'

I squeezed her hand. 'Me too…but we're going to have a proper celebration when I get back! Why don't I book us in to the Sabai restaurant in the city centre. And, who knows, I might even talk you into sharing a small glass of Sauvignon Blanc!'

'Deal,' said Amy switching from sad to happy face.

7

Most Saturdays I like to pop round to see my old friend Marta, especially when we have a little 'business' to attend to. I suggested to Amy that she might like to come along just to get out of her dad's flat for a while and she jumped at the chance. 'As long as you do the talking, Mr Chatterbox, I'll be just fine sitting quietly on the sidelines!'

Amy wanted to buy a few bits and pieces so we agreed to meet at the Greggs corner shop near her flat. Just as she was climbing into the car, I glanced at my phone and noticed that I'd received a text from Marta. It read, 'Looking forward to seeing you. Another batch for you to collect today!' I showed the message to Amy.

'Batch?' she queried.

'This is where you uncover my seamier side!' I said darkly.

'Hmmm. This sounds mysterious,' she said. 'Who is this Marta and … a batch of what? That's what I'm wondering …'

'Yes,' I replied, 'the plot thickens! OK, I'm taking you now to Milton Keynes to meet her.'

'But we're in Milton Keynes …'

'… Ahh, Milton Keynes village—it's tiny and you've probably never even been there. It's the original Milton Keynes and is over a thousand years old. You're going to love it! And you're going to love Marta.'

A few minutes later we pulled into a cute old English village tucked a century away from the bustle of the new city and nestling amongst trees and fields. There were even a couple of cows to add to the perfect rurality of the scene. Amy was very impressed. We drove to the end of the main street, through a set of rusting gates and up a long drive to park outside a large, dilapidated country house.

'Welcome to Marta's place,' I said. 'This is where all the deals get done!'

If Amy was nervous about the prospect of meeting a stranger, I felt confident that Marta's no-nonsense enthusiasm would quickly kick any nerves into the long grass. And so proved to be the case.

Marta is a large, open-hearted and cheerful woman of Polish extraction. Although she's lived in the UK for at least thirty years, her battle with the English language has been one she never looked like winning. Until two years before, she had worked in the university's Law department. But when her husband suddenly died, she retired to concentrate on charity work.

'Peter! Peter, my lovely boy!' She ushered us into her characterful if rather chaotic kitchen. 'And who it is we have here?' she said, turning to Amy with a huge smile.

'This is Amy. We ... we work together,' I said lamely.

'Ooh, and also a clever mathematician, I am betting!' Marta gushed.

'Well, not really,' Amy replied, quickly.

'Ah, I am also thinking modest...and pretty!' Marta was on a roll.

Then Marta pointed to a small cardboard box on the kitchen table.

'Just eight for you this time. I'm sure you can work great magic on them, Peter!'

Amy's curiosity got the better of her. She stepped forward to peep into the box. 'Alarm clocks! I really wasn't expecting that!'

Marta explained. 'I have friend work in house clearance so he get plenty junk that cannot be sold. One strange junk is particularly dead alarm clocks. They are worthless until this genius boy make them fixed!'

Amy frowned. 'But what do you do with all those clocks, Marta?'

'They're to Ukraine. Each week I organise shipment to Kiev. You see, when people lose everything, they still want know time of day.'

'Thanks Marta,' I said. 'I'll get right onto it.'

31

'Are you from Ukraine, then, Marta?' asked Amy.

'No, next one along. I'm Poland but we like to support friends in Ukraine. Look, we have 50 years of Russians *help* us run our country. Now we need to stand by friends who want own independence.'

'Marta helps on other projects as well,' I explained to Amy. '… Women's Aid, Counselling and the Citizen's Advice for example.'

'That's amazing,' said Amy. 'It makes me ashamed that I do nothing!'

'Well, Amy,' Marta replied. 'is not just…altruism. My husband was dead two years past. My children are God-knows-where on other side of world. And here I am rattle around in this big house. I need to fill time being useful somehow!'

'Don't believe her, Amy!' I cut in. 'She does it because she can't stop herself helping people in need. Marta is the kindest person you'll ever meet and with her background in counselling and law, she's an absolute goldmine of useful information!'

Amy beamed a smile at me.

Marta suddenly stared at Amy with a broad grin. 'You're Peter's girlfriend! Why do you not say? But that's just wonderful! I keep telling him to get girlfriend but does he listen…?'

Amy smiled at Marta but wasn't sure how to respond. I jumped in. 'Yes, yes Marta, she *is* my girlfriend!'

She grabbed me in a bear hug and gave me a kiss on both cheeks. 'My lovely boy!' she beamed. Then she moved across to Amy and gave her the same treatment. 'You be nice to him, Amy. This boy is like son to me! You promise?'

Amy smiled at Marta. 'Yes, Marta, I promise. The thing about Pete is … well … he's very easy to love!'

'You're right Amy. That's just it! He easy to love! So, are you living with Peter in his flat?'

Amy blushed slightly. 'No, actually I still…I still live with my father.'

'Well that nice for you then—to be with family.'

Amy took a deep breath. 'Yes, well I suppose it's…quite nice. I suppose it is…'

Marta could sense that she'd perhaps uncovered a can of worms with this topic and quickly changed the subject. Shortly after this we said our goodbyes.

With the cardboard box under my arm, we headed for the car. Driving back to my flat, Amy quickly recovered her mood. Then, to the tune of *We're All Going off to Wembley*, she started singing softly:

'Peter Campbell's girlfriend, I'm Peter Campbell's girlfriend, na na na nah, na na na nah!'

'Hey! That's the first time I've heard you sing! Nice voice!'

'Thank you, sir!' she replied blushing slightly. 'I sing just like Taylor Swift—inside my head, of course!'

'I can't wait to see you work your magic on these old clocks, genius boy!' Amy smiled. When we got back to my flat, she suggested, 'Tell you what—why don't you do tick tock and I'll do chop chop!'

She did a quick whistle stop tour of my fridge. Luckily, I'd done a simple shop the day before. Pulling out a selection of vegetables she announced 'OK then, it's delicious vegetable soup for lunch, I think.'

'Sorry, Amy,' I apologised. 'Not too much there, I fear.'

'Don't worry, there's plenty. And it's all fresh!' she smiled.

'OK, Let's share the kitchen table then.'

I opened a cupboard door and picked up a bag containing the tools of my trade. Pulling out an old sheet, I used it to cover my half of the table's surface and emptied the contents of the cardboard box onto it. But then Amy paused in her cooking. She pulled up a chair and sat down opposite me.

'Actually,' she said with a smile, 'I couldn't possibly concentrate on women's work when I have the opportunity of seeing the boy genius himself perform his magic on these clocks!'

I smiled, sheepishly.

'So, tell me, where did you learn your skills in this field?'

'At the University of the inter-web, I believe,' I replied.

'A three-year course, I assume?' she continued.

'As I remember, it was a 12-minute YouTube video!' I replied. 'The aim here is to get the clocks going—not to trace the complete history of the time machine!'

'OK then, that first one. Talk me through it!'

I picked up a little blue Quartz alarm clock. 'Well, most of the clocks I *fix,* I'm using the term loosely, look like this. And most of them have the same fault—dead battery.' I pulled from my bag a large box of Amazon Basic AAA batteries.

'Now,' I continued, 'what is the procedure again? Ah, yes! Whip out the old battery ... and ... what's next, I wonder? ... oh, I remember now, shove in the new one!'

I held the clock aloft. 'Just listen to that tick, ladies and gentlemen! A quick wipe with a damp cloth ... and it's as good as new!'

Amy clapped vigorously. 'Well done! And if the battery has leaked...?' she asked.

'That's when Plan B kicks into action—the clock goes straight into the bin!'

Amy grinned broadly. 'Now, what about that yellow one? That looks a bit different.'

'Ah, that's an old wind-up travel clock—probably 50 or 60 years old. It doesn't use batteries, which is handy in a country like Ukraine where everything is scarce.'

I looked at the clock's back and checked the winder.

'Overwound, I suspect. But with these old clocks, the oil will have dried out and the goo has gummed up the works.' I carefully opened the back and slowly removed the mechanism. Then I pulled out from my bag a can of Brake Cleaner.

'I'm going to do this bit outside now. The fumes are rather toxic …'

'Ohh! Health and Safety skills as well!' Amy nodded approvingly.

One minute later, the clock was ticking beautifully.

'Wow,' said Amy, 'That was impressive!'

'Well, I still need to lubricate it. I use just a few drops of sewing machine oil for that.'

Ten minutes later I was able to hold the clock aloft and *modestly* wait for the adulation.

'You forgot the damp cloth bit!' Amy laughed.

Half an hour later I had completed all my repairs—well, seven repaired and one in the bin—and Amy had completed her preparations for lunch.

'This *is* cosy!' she giggled.

8

On the following Tuesday, I had a planning meeting in my office with Stacey. Once we had got through her list of agenda items, the mood shifted and we had a bit of a catch up. Her first question was, 'Now Pete, do you know what happened when the world's tongue-twister champion got arrested?'

As a matter of fact, I did know, but I didn't want to spoil her fun. 'Go on then,' I said encouragingly.

'He was given a tough sentence! Terrible, isn't it!'

I smiled at her, enjoying the moment.

'I don't know what you've been doing to our Amy,' Stacey went on. 'She's had a complete personality transplant. She spent lunchtime yesterday telling us all a string of these really corny jokes. She says she got them off some website but she wouldn't tell us what it was.

'Good for her,' I replied happily.

'So, Pete, have you got all your travel arrangements sorted for Stirling?'

'I certainly do, thanks Stacey. I went by car last year but never again! The fast train will get me there in about 6 hours so with the return journey I can get a lot done in 12 hours!'

'I think somebody around here's going to miss you, though!'

I nodded. 'Yea, but it's only one week. Last year I was put down for two weeks on the trot so I can't really complain.'

Stacey patted my hand. 'I'm just so thrilled ... for the pair of you!'

'Thanks, Stacey. Oh, and thanks for your small contribution! Without your guiding hand I'd still be calling her "Amy Who?"!'

'How could you suggest such a thing?!' Stacey laughed.

By far the largest summer school each year in terms of student numbers in the mathematics faculty is the Foundation Course. This is a required one week's residential for first year students to finish off their studies on the basic material and get a chance to think a bit about what course they might move on to next.

The tutors on the residential school are invariably a great bunch of enthusiasts—mostly drawn from a variety of schools, colleges and universities from around the country. As I have often heard them say, it's a joy to be working with students who really want to be here. As one of the permanent members of staff, I am expected to assume the role of Course Director. I've always seen my main task as one of supporting nervous students, particularly through those first few potentially lonely days. I've found that, after they've spent a year studying on their own, it is actually easy to get them chatting to their fellow students who are making a similar journey.

In the opening welcome session, I started by inviting everyone to look around the theatre and take in the other 250 or so strangers with whom they will be sharing their lives over the next 7 days. 'A bit of a funny-looking bunch, aren't they!' I said. This got a nervous laugh and was a useful ice-breaker. But I followed this up by saying that on the final day I'll be asking them to do the same exercise.

'By next Friday, you'll be looking at the same people but they won't be a funny-looking bunch at all. Quite the reverse! One week from now, you'll recognise most of the faces. You'll have met and chatted to many of them and you'll be seeing them as real people who have lives, challenges, fears and aspirations similar to your own. You'll hear about their everyday problems, like trying to get time off work to attend a tutorial or having to get up at 2AM to work on an assignment because the kids won't leave them alone during the day.'

Already I could see my audience starting to relax. They recognised these scenarios and were beginning to believe that they might actually enjoy the next seven days in the company of these 'funny-looking' strangers.

'Do you mind if I join you?' I said to a woman sitting on her own drinking a coffee. 'No, please do,' she smiled, moving her bag and coat off a chair to make room.

'I'm Pete,' I said, setting down my sandwich and offering a handshake.

'Oh, I know that,' she replied. 'I've just seen your one-man show—you're a very funny man! I'm Meg—one of those nervous first-timers you were just talking about in the lecture.'

I nodded. 'So, what made nervous Meg decide to turn her life upside down and enrol on a university maths course?'

Meg laughed. 'Well, it wasn't because I love maths or was ever even good at it at school. It was a family thing; just something that happened last year.'

I raised my eyebrows and waited.

'Well, the truth is I hated school. The teachers always managed to make me feel stupid. Maths lessons were particularly depressing—most of the time I didn't know what was going on but I was always too scared to ask!'

I smiled encouragingly. 'I get the picture!'

'Anyway, one weekend last year I was dropping my daughter off to start her degree course at Sheffield University. We carried in her bags and within 20 minutes, Kirsten had already met four of the other students on her corridor— chat, chat, chat. Then she was heading off to the shared kitchen area with them for a coffee, with barely a backward glance. I *so* envied her!...and I just decided then and there to get out and do something similar for myself.'

'Good for you,' I replied. 'And, one year on, do you still feel stupid?'

'Definitely not!' Meg replied animatedly. 'I just love it all. The course materials are so clear and well designed. If I get stuck, it's all there in the units and if I still don't get it, well my tutor is fantastic. It's a whole different world from school!'

That evening in the bar, I found myself sitting beside Dermot, a tall fisherman from Donegal. It was a real delight just to listen to him talk—he had that slow, hypnotic, dreamy style of delivery so characteristic of people from the West coast of Ireland. I sat quietly while Dermot described his typical day—how he brings his maths study units along in his boat just on the off-chance that he might be able to slot in half an hour or so while he's waiting for the fish to find their way into his nets. He was in the mood to talk so I just let him. To my great pleasure, I could clearly hear my parents' voices and accent in his words as he spoke. Although the counties of Donegal and Tyrone are contained within two different national jurisdictions, they still share membership of the nine counties that comprise Ulster. Sitting listening to him describe his world did make me feel nostalgic about …something. But I wasn't quite sure what.

When I travel to summer school, I always bring my guitar. There's usually a bit of a sing-song in the bar and on Thursday night the tutors can be relied upon to put on some sort of musical entertainment for the students. Just describing it makes it all sound a bit corny and clichéd but in reality, it is good fun that even the most hard-bitten cynic finds themselves enjoying. (It's a case of, *you had to be there* …!) After all the shenanigans and conversations had been completed, it was after 11pm before I was able to call it a night.

I had been able to send Amy a couple of short texts through the day and she had sent me a prompt reply each time. But the FaceTime call that I'd promised on her laptop was later than planned. I knew that she'd be really pleased to hear from me—and she was— but I could also see from her body language and hear from her voice that she wasn't quite her usual bubbly self. She asked me about my day. After I'd gone through the main events, I asked her what she'd been up to.

'Let me see?' she said. 'Now did I get around to giving that big keynote speech in the Lecture Theatre. Nope … cancelled! Oh yes and my glockenspiel recital in the Campus Bar after work. No … sadly that didn't happen either. Ah, but I did watch a bit of TV with my dad and then it was back to my bedroom to read. So, all in all, a pretty eventful day!'

I could see that she was a bit low in spirits. 'Could you do with a bit more adventure in your life, I wonder?' I asked. Amy looked away. She was quiet for a moment and then stared at me and nodded.

'Well, if you think you could shoehorn another event into your busy social calendar, Miss Carpenter, do you think you might give serious consideration to some sort of an outing with me?'

This time I got a hint of a smile.

'Leave it with me, Aims. I've got a little idea...!'

9

When I returned to Milton Keynes the following Saturday afternoon, I found a small bunch of sweet peas waiting for me on the doorstop. They had been kept damp with a couple of sheets of wet kitchen roll, wrapped in kitchen foil. It was all tied with ribbon and attached to a home-made card with a red heart on one side and the words "Missed you!, A xx" on the other. I pictured in my mind the effort she would have had to have made to put this little home-coming gift together and then have it waiting for me by my front door. It was not something that Clare would ever have thought of doing, or indeed ever did in the twelve years we'd been together.

I was suddenly filled with an emotional wave of love and protectiveness about Amy. I realised how much I had missed her over the previous seven days. Putting the flowers into a vase with water, I snapped them with my phone and sent the photo as an attachment along with an email. The text consisted of a lyric from one of the songs that Amy had included in her Top 25 Playlist, Taylor Swift's 'Jump Then Fall'.

"Take a deep breath and jump then fall into me.

'Cause every time you smile, I smile.

And every time you shine, I'll shine for you."

Five minutes later my laptop was buzzing. A welcome home FaceTime from Amy, no doubt. Indeed it was Amy but to my surprise, it was sad-face Amy who presented herself on my screen.

'Thanks so much, Pete' That Taylor Swift quote was ju … so lovely.' She started to sob gently.

41

'Blimey, Aims, if I'd have thought it would have had this effect, I'd never have sent it!'

Now she was sobbing and laughing at the same time.

'I'm so sorry, Pete,' she managed to blurt out. Then there was silence. I could see that if ever there was a time for a grand gesture, this was it.

'Hey, Amy. Do you know what you're going to be doing this evening?'

She shook her head.

'I'll tell you, then. You're going to look through the glad rags hanging in your wardrobe and find something devastating to put on. Slap on a dash of that perfume you were wearing the day I became your 'ero at the Marina roundabout. Then you'll be taken to the Sabai restaurant for a fabulous romantic date with the man of your dreams!'

She smiled … well, it was almost a smile. 'Am I?' she replied quietly.

'OK, I'm booking it now. I'll be picking you up at 6.30 and then we can have a nice meal followed by a proper conversation.'

Silence. 'OK then Pete. That would be really lovely.'

'Bye for now.'

'Bye, Pete. See you at the corner shop at 6.30! Oh and Pete, I can't tell you what it means to have someone to shine for me. Thank you.'

That evening, Amy and I were seated together in the Sabai Restaurant in the city centre—in a way, only our second proper date along with the Canny Band concert. As soon as she'd sat down, she started fidgeting in her chair and I knew that she was still in a state of nervous agitation. She sighed uneasily.

'Amy, I was wondering. Are you OK with us … erm … spending so much time together?'

She gave me a look of horror. 'Of course I am. I just love being with you. Please believe me about that. This has all been … well, you know!'

'But …?' I probed.

'But … it's just … oh, my mind is in a muddle. I don't know where to start. My whole life is a total mess!'

I was really shocked. 'Amy—I'm so sorry to hear that!' Then, when she'd collected her thoughts, she began to speak. 'I just need to tell you something …something important about me.' She paused.

'Good evening, madam, sir. Can I give you your menus?' The smiling waiter handed us each a huge leather-bound tome. 'In the meantime, perhaps you'd like to order some drinks?' He smiled at Amy encouragingly. She shook her head and lowered it to give the tablecloth a closer inspection. He then turned to me. 'Sir?'

'Oh, OK, I'll just have a small glass of Sauvignon Blanc, please.'

The waiter looked back in Amy's direction but she wasn't having any of it. She shook her head once more and said quietly, 'Just water will be fine.'

He departed and there was a short silence before Amy raised her eyes to look at me. 'Go on Aims,' I said encouragingly. 'You were saying…that you wanted to tell me something.'

Amy took a deep breath. 'OK, it's just…I think you should know…that the Amy you thought you knew is really … is really a total phoney!'

I kissed her hand and smiled, waiting for her to continue.

She took her hand away. 'Oh Pete, I just feel so ashamed.'

'Ashamed about what?'

'About…about lying to you. All last week while you were in Stirling I just lay awake each night thinking about it.'

'I don't understand. When did you lie to me?'

'Well, let me give you some examples.' Amy paused to compose her thoughts.

'Your wine, sir.' The waiter set down my glass. In his other hand he was carrying a carafe of iced water from which he topped up Amy's glass. He filled my glass and set down the carafe. 'Enjoy!' he beamed at us. 'I'll be back in a few minutes to take your order.'

'Hey, Aims,' I said after he had departed. 'In the interest of speeding things along, last time I was here I had a Chicken Mussaman Curry with rice and I had some fried aubergines with it.

43

It was bloomin' lovely. When he comes back, shall we order two of those?'

She gave me a brief smile. 'Thanks, Pete. That sounds perfect!'

'But meanwhile,' I went on. 'You were about to surprise me with some examples of when you…lied to me?'

She nodded. 'Well, here's an example. Do you remember when we had that first get-together in the Campus bar? You offered to buy me a drink and my response was to say it was a 'bit early for a proper drink'.

'Oh yes, I remember…'

'And then later you give me a bottle of something alcoholic—a bottle of Bud. Well, I… I just pretended to drink it. That whole thing was make-believe. I've never really drunk any alcohol in my life.'

I took her hand again. 'Not a very big lie though!'

'It was still a lie Pete! And there was another time when you asked me if I'd travelled much. "Oh yes," I replied. I suddenly remembered that I'd been visiting sunny Italy here and skiing in the Alps there. How I just *love* skiing! None of it true! I've never been anywhere!'

I nodded. 'OK …'

'And remember when you asked me out for our first date you wanted to know the last time I'd been to a music concert? I told you some story about a concert I went to in Birmingham…with a friend. What friend was that, I wonder? The truth is I'd never ever been to a music concert in my whole life.'

Amy sat staring at the table and I gave her hand another squeeze. 'Again, not much of a lie though.'

'I was being dishonest, Pete. And you deserve better than that!'

'But can I just ask, Aims…these are such silly little lies. Why couldn't you simply tell me the truth?'

'Because…because I just wanted you to like me and…and I didn't want you to think that I was some sort of no-life weirdo loser.'

Suddenly the smiling waiter was standing by our table once more, ready for action. 'Hello again! Now, can I take your orders?'

I smiled back at him. 'Yes, we'll both have the same, please. That's two Chicken Mussaman Curries with rice and some fried aubergines as a side dish.'

The waiter nodded. 'Certainly sir,' he replied and disappeared back to the kitchen area.

After a long pause, I said, 'Well Amy. I'm very glad you've got that worry off your chest. I can see that it has really upset you but, honestly, it hasn't upset me. I'd just like to say, please don't twist yourself into knots to make me like you. Because, guess what, I like you as you are! From now on let's always be honest with each other.'

I had hoped that this response might have helped to lift Amy's mood but from her expression I could see that I was wrong. 'Is there more, Aims? In this new era of honesty, please just say it!'

'OK,' she replied, slowly. 'Yes, there is more. I want to tell you about…my dad. Ever since my mum died it's just been the two of us—me and dad, dad and me. The "gruesome twosome", he calls us. "We're a team, Amy. As long as we stick together nothing bad can ever happen to us".'

'But that's nice, isn't it Aims. It sounds like he really cares about you.'

She paused as she composed her thoughts.

'He does love me. I know he does. And I love him. But…'

There was a long pause. I smiled at her encouragingly.

'…but sometimes it feels…just too much.'

'In what way?' I asked gently.

'I feel…that he just clings on to me so tightly and never wants to let me go. I don't feel I can have friends or any social life at all really. He's always going "Oh, you don't want to be doing that, Amy! You've got everything you need here!"'

'So, what's actually missing in your life?'

I want to be independent of him so that I can…make my own choices and not have to run them past him every time. All the time I'm feeling that he wouldn't cope on his own without me and it's so…exhausting!'

45

'And what about your dad? Does he have friends or a social life of his own?'

'No! That's just it. He's a real loner and all of his social needs are just…are just piled onto me. I find it totally suffocating. It just makes me want to run away.'

I thought about these dilemmas for a while and then said 'So why don't you? What's actually stopping you from running away from him and starting your own life without him.'

Amy looked at me sadly. 'Well, that raises another issue that I feel trapped by. Of the two of us, I'm the only one earning any real money. It's my money that pays the rent. It's my money that pays the bills and the groceries. Without me I sometimes think he'd be…on the streets.'

My eyes widened in amazement. 'Wow, Amy, this is…crazy! It's just plain wrong that he has this hold over you. You shouldn't feel surprised that you feel suffocated by him…because you are. You're an adult and you don't need to be controlled!'

'So here we are then,' said our waiter, wheeling a trolley of steaming dishes and plates. For this visit he was accompanied by a nervous-looking young waitress who busied herself rearranging our table to make room for the food.

The waiter picked up the side dishes and placed them tenderly onto the spaces she had created. 'Your rice, and your aubergine side dishes.'

'Thanks, thanks very much,' I said.

The waitress then picked up our napkins, unrolled them and began gently placing them on our laps.

'Thanks…that's fine…thank you.'

Next the waiter carefully placed our main dishes before us. 'So, two Chicken Mussaman Curries'.

'Thanks, thanks very much,' I said yet again.

I looked across at Amy. She seemed smaller than I'd remembered her…or was it just that she'd sunk a few inches deeper into her chair? Then the waitress picked up the rice dish along with one of the serving spoons and started heading in the direction of Amy's empty plate.

'No, no,' I interjected with a smile. 'No, really, we can take it from here. Thank you. Thank you both very much. It all looks...lovely.'

Our waitress seemed a little disappointed at being deprived of one of her main serving tasks so I treated her to an especially warm grin. 'Enjoy!' said the waiter. Both gave us a smiling bow and retreated to the kitchen area.

The smell was every bit as exquisite as I'd remembered from my last visit and I was delighted to see Amy enthusiastically piling on generous portions of rice and aubergines onto her plate. After a few minutes of silent eating, she finally said, 'Pete this is delicious. And these aubergines are just, what's the word?'

'Yum?' I suggested.

'That's it,' she laughed. 'Yum!'

Amy was starting to relax now and the confessions of her sins of perfidy and her father's controlling behaviour both took a backseat as she tucked into the curry. I topped up her glass of water and filled another for myself.

When we had eventually taken a pause from eating, she flashed me a warm and happy smile. 'Thanks so much, Pete. This is really great. I'm so happy to be here with you and this meal is...well, it's just fantastic!'

I grinned at her. 'Hurray! Glad to get you back again. I missed you, AC! But you were going through some of the things that were wrong in your life.'

She nodded slowly. And it all began pouring out. 'Because I've never got out into the world, there are so many things I've never done. I don't have a passport, I can't swim, I can't ride a bike, and of course I can't drive a car. I'm pretty useless actually. Look, I'm sitting here in a fancy restaurant with you. This is something I never do—I've no idea how to order food or drinks or anything like that. I feel that I'm just sitting on the edge of the world, looking in.'

'And this is all because ...?'

'Well, my shyness hasn't helped—I know that. But I'm now starting to see just how much my dad has been a part of it. You see, all the normal things that parents encourage their children to be able

47

to do…to function as an adult, well, he never did. My dad is… a puzzle,' Amy sighed. 'I can't even tell him about you. I think he might be incredibly jealous—like I've betrayed him. I just don't … I don't trust him with that information.'

I thought about all these issues for a moment. 'It's not right, Aims. Would you like me to see if I can help you with some of them?'

Amy looked unsure. 'I do appreciate the offer, Pete. We really have a fantastic relationship … all in just a few weeks and I still can't believe it … but I don't want to … I don't want to lose all that by becoming something that you feel you need to fix. I'd hate to be the … the let's-fix-Amy project!'

'Yes, I can see that. But please believe me when I say I don't want to fix you. As far as I'm concerned, you're perfect. The problem is the stuff that surrounds you. Look, if I could grant you two wishes today, what would you really like to happen to make your life better?'

Amy considered the question carefully.

'One, I'd like to …I'd like to be fully in control of my own money and spend it how I like. And two … I'm twenty three, for God's sake. I'd like to be having SEX!' At that moment the middle-aged couple at the adjacent table paused their conversation. The woman glanced at us in a disapproving manner while her husband winked at me. I patted Amy's hand. 'You wouldn't like to repeat that last comment a bit louder, madam,' I said to her quietly. 'There's a woman sitting at the far side of the restaurant complaining that she didn't quite hear it!' Luckily Amy could see the funny side of this scenario and we both dissolved into giggles.

There were a few moments of reflective silence before Amy continued. 'There are two more things that I've been thinking about while you've been off larking about at summer school.'

'Gosh,' I said with a smile. 'You've certainly been doing a lot of thinking while I've been away!'

She laughed.

'Well, take that touch phobia that I thought I had. It turns out that four quick Salsa classes later it seems to have disappeared. How do you explain that? Then, of course, there's my shyness. If there's anything that defines poor Amy in the eyes of the world it's that she's very, very shy. Well, what if my shyness turns out to be just a habit that I've let myself get into. I'm now thinking, sod it! I'm fed up being that shy person. Maybe, with a bit of help from Cheeky Chappie Peter Campbell … just maybe I don't need to be her anymore.'

I smiled encouragingly at her. 'Well, I think I can speak for Cheeky Chappie Pete and he says he's all in. You and me together— let's try to fix some of these things that are making you unhappy. If you ever feel I'm going in too hard, just say and I'll back off.'

Amy's face softened and she said, 'I'd really like that, if you could bear it.'

'My dear young lady, it would be a delight to work with you on this exciting collaborative project!'

Amy responded with a grin.

'OK then, Amy. Now I've got a proposition that I'd like to make. And I really hope you will say yes.'

She looked at me with a little apprehension. I could see *what's coming now* written in her eyes.

'It's relevant to what we've just been talking about. You may remember last Saturday evening when I was at summer school and we chatted on FaceTime?'

She nodded.

'At the time you said that you were looking for more adventure in your life.'

She nodded again, slightly more slowly this time.

'I told you then that I might have a plan. Well, here it is. I'd really like you to go away with me this coming weekend?'

Amy carefully set down her fork and stared blankly.

'I'm serious. But don't ask where; it's a surprise.'

She thought for a while and then said, 'I hope you're not taking me off into the unknown just to … you know, jump me!'

'Now Amy,' I replied, 'You know I'd never do that!'

49

Amy smiled and patted my hand. 'Well, I do really!'

'However,' I continued, 'if *you* were to decide to try to "jump" *me*, as you so delicately put it, then that would be a different matter.'

'What do you mean?' Amy asked innocently.

'Well, let me put it in simple terms. If, over the course of our weekend of fun, you were seriously thinking about engaging in a spot of "jumping", well, I'd like to assure you that I definitely wouldn't be … unmoved by your blandishments.'

Amy laughed out loud. 'My blandishments!'

'And I can't speak plainer than that!' I added.

After a short pause, Amy continued. 'All blandishments aside, however …, I'd still like to know where you're taking me.'

I shook my head slowly. 'Nope!'

Amy shrugged. 'Well, I'll have to lie to my dad, of course, but I've been getting good at that, recently! So, let's say yes!'

'OK then. It's a deal! I think I like this new sod-it-let's-just-do-it Amy even better than the old one!'

Amy looked at her watch. 'Oh God, is that the time. I said I'd be home half an hour ago!'

I quickly paid the bill and ran her back in my car. At Amy's request I dropped her off on the street adjacent to her home.

'Thanks Pete. Oh, and before I go, could I just ask you to close your eyes and pucker up?'

I did as I was told. She leaned over and gave me a long hard kiss on the mouth.

'Thanks,' she smiled. 'I need as much practice as I can get, especially if you're determined to drag me off for this dirty weekend!'

She jumped out of the car and ran off in the direction of home.

10

'Now then Amy, you don't seem to have grasped the whole notion of a surprise.'

'Just a little hint then. Please!'

'OK, I'll tell you three things. First, we'll be there in about thirty minutes. Second, you're going to like it—I'm certain of that. And third ... well, I think I've just forgotten what the third was. Oh, did I say you're going to like it. That must have been it!'

I changed the subject. 'Anyway, how's the bus thing with Marcie working out?'

Amy made a face. 'I'd love a better arrangement,' she replied.

'Imagine an alternative universe where you owned a bike and were able to ride it,' I continued. 'Would you go for that option?'

Amy nodded enthusiastically. 'Like a shot! Actually, I've checked out the MK Redway network—you know, the red paths exclusively for cycles—and they practically run from home to work, door to door.'

'And if we could find a way to help make that happen, would you, erm, ...'

'...I'd give this particular collaborative project a very positive double thumbs up,' she interrupted.

We sat quietly for a few minutes, watching the motorway eat up the miles. 'So, how did dad take the news about your weekend adventure?'

Amy suddenly looked more serious. 'The thing about my dad is, you always need to be prepared. The golden rule—always anticipate what his objections are going to be and then be sure to have everything in place.'

'He didn't take it well then?'

Amy laughed. 'Of course not! His first response was to be furious—what am I going to eat, I can't afford takeaway every evening, and all that. So, I opened the freezer and showed him the three meals I'd prepared for him labelled Friday, Saturday and Sunday.'

I smiled at her. 'Hmm ... *and* Sunday? Long weekend planned, then?'

'As if I would know!' she countered. 'Anyway, then he started ranting about it all being ridiculously last minute. That's when I had to pull out my Ace of trumps and show him the official documentation.'

'Really? And where did that come from?'

'My handbag!'

Amy reached into her handbag and pulled out a rather official-looking letter.

'Hmm, nice headed paper. Looks the business!' I said.

Amy read it out to me.

Dear Ms Carpenter,

We are delighted to welcome you to the first of a series of required weekend courses on the theme of Relationships and the Workplace. The course has national approval and has been organised by the DWA. The first three study themes are:

1. *Getting to Know You*

2. *Peeling Back the Layers*, and

3. *The Circle of Trust*.

Further details of the sessions can be found in the text messages that you should have already received.

Yours,

Pat O'Hagen (organiser)

Then she returned the letter to her bag.

I began to smile. 'Wow! Impressive stuff. I wonder what DWA stands for.'

'Well, good question, Mr Campbell. I believe it's *Developing Workplace Attitudes.*'

'Mmm, that's sounds important!' I smiled in response. And there was me thinking it referred to…Dirty Weekends Away.'

'Ha ha!' Amy replied. 'I wouldn't have expected anything less from you!'

'Anyway, this is all brilliant!' I continued. 'And did I see that it's not one but *three* weekend courses?'

'Oh at the very least. There may be more. You can never get too much … erm … self-improvement.'

As soon as we'd left the M1, she started calling out the names of the towns on the road signs. 'Rugby, Coventry, Warwick. Oh Warwick. Are we going there?'

I said nothing.

'Well, I know were headed north.' Amy went into full commentary mode.

'Hmm, this is a bit different! Oh, that sign says Cotswold country. Are we headed for the Cotswolds then? Look, Cotswold stone. I'm getting excited now. Is it a pub, or a B&B? Or maybe a camping site …'

A few minutes later, Amy read out 'Chipping Campden! I think I've heard of that. Or was that Chipping Norton? What happens here then?'

We swung along the main street and I parked the car on the road opposite an old cottage. Amy looked across to see two smiling faces peering out from one of the windows.

'What's going on, Pete?' said Amy, suddenly looking ill at ease. 'Where the hell have you brought…'

Suddenly, two small boys came clattering out of a half-shuttered door. 'They're here, they're here! Hello Uncle Pete. Hello Amy!' They grabbed Amy's hands and dragged her unwillingly into the kitchen. 'She's here, she's here!' they shouted to their mum and dad who looked on helplessly. 'Where are your bags? Come on, come and see our bedroom. Do you want to see where you're sleeping?' Then as they ran past a hamster in a cage, 'Oh, this is Mario!'

'Boys, boys, calm down. Amy needs to be introduced properly.' I tried my best to exercise some order amidst the chaos. Amy didn't really know what had just hit her. Her eyes were wide in amazement and not a little fear as she was being dragged from room to room.

I was about to intervene and rescue her when Sam suddenly stopped, looked at her closely and asked 'Amy, do you know about *us*?' Gradually, Amy began to recover her wits. 'Let's see,' she replied slowly. 'Uncle Pete has told me a few things. I think he said your real names were…the Chuckle Boys'.

'No, no,' they chorused.

'That's our website!' added Harry.

'Oh—OK then,' Amy went on. 'Apparently there are two jokers who live here … called Sam and Harry.'

'Yes, that's us. We're the jokers!' shouted Sam.

'What else? What else do you know?'

Amy looked blank. I decided to intervene.

'What about that chicken, Amy?' I suggested.

She stared back at me with incomprehension. Then suddenly the light bulb in her brain switched on.

'Hmm, what else do I know?' she repeated. 'Well, I also know…why the chicken crossed the playground.'

'To get to the other slide!' both boys shouted together with great enthusiasm.

Amy then turned to the two smiling adults in the room. 'Amy! We're so pleased to meet you!' said Annie. 'We're Annie and Ben! Welcome!'

Amy extended an arm for a handshake but both of her hosts opted for a warm hug instead.

'Now Amy,' said Annie, 'just to say that we've got only one guest room so you and Pete'll be sharing. Are you OK with that?'

Amy smiled shyly and nodded.

'Are you sure?' Annie persisted.

Amy glanced across at me and then said, 'I'm fine, Annie. But … thanks for asking.'

'OK then,' said Annie. 'Sit down, sit down and I'll make some tea.'

Amy did as instructed. Almost immediately, Sam climbed onto her knee, wrapped his arms tightly around her neck and said into her ear in a loud stage whisper, 'Are you excited about tomorrow?'

Amy smiled. 'What's happening tomorrow?'

'You know, with the bike,' he whispered.

'The bike? The thing is, Sam, this is my special surprise weekend and I'VE BEEN TOLD NOTHING! Do you hear that, Peter Campbell? I said, Nothing at all!'

'OK, Amy,' I said, finally. 'Time for full disclosure. We have been lucky enough to secure the services of the two best cycling instructors in all of Chipping Campden ...'

The boys jumped to attention.

'... and tomorrow they will be teaching you ... how to ride a bicycle!'

Both boys jumped up and down excitedly and clapped their hands.

'Are you very excited, Amy?' Ben asked her.

Amy's eyes widened. 'I, I just can't tell you how much.' she managed to say.

11

That evening, when the boys had gone to bed, the four of us sat down around the dinner table.

'So, Pete,' Annie asked. 'Have you seen much of mum and dad recently?'

'Well, I ring them every Sunday, of course but...I guess it's been 5 or 6 weeks since I got back home to see them.'

'Yea, well we managed to get down to Leamington about three weekends ago,' responded Annie. 'They just love to see the boys, of course.'

'So how did you find them?' I asked. 'On the phone they sound just like themselves but I think dad's mobility's not so hot these days.'

'No, you're right there. He really needs a new pair of knees but he won't hear about getting them done.'

'Why not?'

Well,' continued Annie, 'his excuse is that what with mum's angina he sees himself as her carer, which to be fair he is these days, but he says he won't abandon her while he's recuperating from the op.'

'Do you think maybe he's also a bit nervous about...going under the knife?' Ben remarked.

'Oh, I'm sure there'd be a bit of that too,' I agreed.

'Well, I've offered to have them both up here for those few weeks but of course they won't hear tell of it! Oh, Pete, I forgot to tell you. Dad came up with another joke for the boys' website.'

'OK, fire away,' I smiled back at her.

'Urm,' said Annie uncertainly. 'Now, what was it again, Ben?'

'I think it was the one about...the piece of cake?'

'Oh yes,' Annie smiled. 'That was it! Why did Sam eat his homework?'

'I don't know. Why did Sam eat his homework?' I responded, playing along.

'Because his teacher said it would be a piece of cake!'

'Ha ha, great!' I replied. 'That's a little parcel of chucklesome perfection!' I turned to Amy who had been observing the conversation quietly from the sidelines. 'Now, Aims, you've got a fresh young mind that remembers things. Can you log that one in please until we get back?'

Amy smiled and nodded assent.

Then Ben turned to Amy. 'Oh Amy, we've been very rude. When this Campbell twosome get together nobody else gets a look in.'

Amy smiled nervously.

'What about your family, Amy?' Ben went on. 'Do you have brothers or sisters?'

Amy reddened slightly. 'No…no, my family's nothing like yours. I come from…a very small family.'

Ben seemed to sense that Amy wasn't entirely comfortable talking about her family so decided to include her into the conversation by taking a different path.

'So, Pete tells us that you're a secretary in the same faculty as him.

Amy nodded.

'And have you always been a secretary?'

'Not always,' she replied, quietly. 'At eighteen I went to Warwick University but I left at the end of the first year.'

This was news to me so I listened with great interest as Annie took over the interview.

'Oh, that's a shame.' Annie added.

Amy nodded, reddening a little.

'So why did you leave, Amy?' Ben continued.

Amy paused, seemingly not sure how to answer.

'My dad got ill.'

'Oh dear. What was his illness?' Ben asked.

There was a long pause while Amy stared at the table. Eventually she shook her head. 'I don't know.'

It was clear at this point that the interrogation was over and eventually it was Amy who broke the silence. Looking at both Annie and Ben in turn she asked, 'Anyway, what do you two do? Something very high-powered, I'm sure.'

Annie laughed 'Well, if you call being a primary school teacher high-powered then yes, that's definitely me!'

'Gosh, you've got your hands full then Annie, what with the boys and everything…'

'…Oh, I just do mornings these days. That's plenty for me! But the best bit is I'm available for the holidays which is a real boon!'

Amy turned to Ben. 'And what about you Ben?'

He drew his wallet from his pocket, pulled out a little green business card and slid it across the table in Amy's direction.

'Ben Wilson Landscape Gardeners at your service, madam. If you ever need a hedge trimmed or your lawn re-turfed or even a bit of decking in the back garden, I'm your man!'

'Well, I'll certainly keep your card in a safe place, Ben, but please don't expect an immediate response!'

Well done, Amy—I mused. I think you danced around that conversation pretty well! But maybe it's time to make some moves now in the direction of bed.

'Well, guys, this Cotswolds ozone is starting to get to me. And these dishes won't wash themselves.' I began clearing them up. Everyone pitched in and in no time everything had been wiped down with the dishwasher loaded.

'Oh Amy,' said Ben suddenly. 'Please don't worry about the bike lessons. It'll be great. We have a pretty foolproof system here. The village green is just around the corner. It has a gentle hill so you can start on the mound, then roll down it on your bike without having to pedal. That way you can learn to balance the bike without having to worry about keeping the wheels turning. You'll be cycling in no time, and the boys will keep you right!'

'Thanks for the encouragement!' said Amy, still looking rather nervous about it all. 'I'm sure I'll be … fine!'

'Well, I think it's bedtime for me,' I said.

'Me too', said Amy, giving my hand a secret squeeze.

'I've told the boys not before seven. Then they'll be in bed beside you, I'm afraid. Hope you don't mind four in a bed, Amy.'

'Oh no problem—I'm so used to that,' smiled Amy.

Fifteen minutes later, we were in bed together, touching noses. 'Hey Amy,' I whispered. 'Sorry about the third degree from Ben. Sometimes he can be a bit…you know…relentless!'

Amy put her arms around my neck and kissed me. 'No, it was fine. I'm OK knowing that you'll be there to rescue me if things get a bit sticky!'

'Hey, Aims, you know all that stuff about Warwick University and having to come home because your dad was ill?'

'I do,' she replied.

'Well…I knew nothing about any of that.'

'I know. It's something I never talk about.'

'Do you mind talking to *me* about it?'

There was a pause before she replied. 'I'd be happy to talk to you about it, but I'm not quite up to a *public* performance.'

'Fair enough. Well, can I ask you, about your dad. What happened there?'

'Well, he was hospitalised and couldn't really look after himself. I had to come back to take care of him.'

'What was his illness?'

'He didn't fully get to the bottom of that. But…but he says his health was never the same afterwards.'

'What a shame. OK, next question—what did you study at Warwick?'

'French. I just loved it. I always seemed to find it easy because … well …'

'Wow!' I interrupted. 'Your French is really amazing so that explains a lot.'

She laughed. 'So…if ever you want French lessons, Mr Campbell, just knock on my door!'

I smiled at her. 'Well, that's really good to hear. Talking of which, when we were at that restaurant and I offered you two wishes, can you remember what your second one was?'

Amy giggled. 'Of course I do, you big sexpot!'

'Well…' I began.

'Well,' she interrupted, 'if you're asking if I'm up for it, the answer is yes! But not here. Can we wait 'til we're back at your place—on Sunday night?'

'Hmmm,' I replied. 'That sounds like a premium plan! But to use a cycling metaphor, are you comfortable with going from zero to 50mph in five seconds?'

'I am,' she whispered.

'Seriously though, any worries?'

She paused before answering. 'Well, if I'm to be totally honest …'

'You must!'

'Well, when it comes to SEX, there are two little things that might worry me a bit,' she continued.

'Which are?'

'Which are … one, will it hurt and, two, well, you need to know that I'm not on any sort of contraception.'

'Hmm. Those are actually two very big things. I promise you that with careful planning we'll…get those two things right. As I've often heard Sam say, *teamwork makes the dream work!*'

Amy nodded. 'Thanks Pete,' she whispered. 'Teamwork it is, then!'

'OK,' I went on. 'But in the meantime, there are some important osculatory skills that we still haven't covered.'

Amy raised her eyebrows. 'Does that mean what I think it means?'

'Probably!' I continued. 'Tonight, I'd like to show you the legendary *kiss à la mode française.*'

'Oh, that sounds *très exotique.* And what does that involve, exactly?'

'As before, lick your lips but this time, part them slightly. Now, prepare yourself for *un petit visiteur.*'

Two minutes later, Amy said, 'Oh I really like this *à la mode française*. So, that one was *chez moi*. Please lick and part your lips now … and prepare for a return visit, *chez toi*.'

We spent a long time giving these more advanced osculatory skills a thorough workout until, exhausted, we fell asleep in each other's arms.

12

'So, do you hear much from *madam* these days?'

Annie had never been Clare's greatest fan and since her departure to the USA a year earlier had been finding it increasingly difficult to refer to her by name.

'Now and again. She's incredibly busy of course, with her new job …'

'… Oh, I'm sure!' Annie interrupted. 'Incredibly busy! I bet *it's been just crazy here*!' The last five words were pronounced scornfully and in an exaggerated American accent.

I thought for a moment. 'We did have some good times together, though.'

'Yea, but you're using the past tense. Be honest, love. There haven't been really good times with *herself* for years!'

'I guess so,' I replied thoughtfully.

'Well, you know what mum would say about her—that she's very good to herself! To be brutally honest, the only person Clare ever cared about was … Clare! But who cares! Just ditch the bitch! You've got Amy now and I just say Yippee! And so does Ben, by the way! We really like her. What a breath of fresh air! Yes, she's a bit shy but she has…a lovely nature and a kind heart. And for some weird reason she seems to really like you!'

I laughed. 'Thanks. That means a lot! Yea, I was a bit nervous that she wouldn't speak—this shyness thing—but …'

Annie laughed. '… the boys never gave her a chance, did they! Just look at the three of them now!'

We were sitting on a bench by the village green. Amy was cycling on the grass on Annie's old bike with Sam running alongside shouting encouragement.

'Great, you're doing great, you're going to beat it!'

Harry was on the mound using the stopwatch on his mum's phone and shouting out the time in seconds, 'Five … ten…fifteen …'

Annie laughed. 'I think she's gonna make it. Don't you?'

I smiled. 'Do you mean as a cyclist or as a future life partner?'

'Both, I hope!' Annie replied. 'It certainly looks like she's getting the hang of it. My two little cycling geniuses are doing a fantastic job!'

Annie pointed, 'Look, she's actually pedalling now, *and* still staying up.'

Amy looked over at us, saw that we were watching and took one hand off the handlebars to give a confident wave. She immediately hit a wobble and fell over … again. The boys swooped in, helped her to her feet and they all went back up to the top of the mound.

Then Annie caught my arm. 'Hey, why didn't you tell me about Amy before, you big eejit?'

I shrugged. 'Because … because there wasn't a before.'

'Hmmph, great answer! Can you rephrase that into a meaningful sentence please!'

'Well,' I continued, 'I've really only known Amy a few weeks.'

'Rubbish, sure don't you two work together!'

'Yes, we do. We even have offices in the same faculty building and on the same floor but … I suppose … I hadn't really noticed her.'

'Ha! But had she noticed you?'

'I think so,' I smiled 'but,' I shrugged, '… you know …'

'Yea, she was too shy to move in on you and you were too stupid to see it!'

'Something like that,' I conceded.

Fifteen minutes later, Annie and I were standing up and clapping furiously as a little gang of three cyclists were doing giant figures-of-eight on the grass. The boys were cheering and Amy was grinning from ear to ear. We went over to them and Annie shouted 'Well done, Amy. You're now a member of the family cycling team!' Then she said 'OK guys; who's for a drink and a biscuit?'

We walked back to the cottage. Amy was still breathing hard, red-cheeked and hair sticking out everywhere. I gave her a kiss on the cheek. 'Brilliant, AC! Well done you!'

'Yes,' she agreed. 'But my team is everything. If I'm ever to cycle on the roads, I'll need them there with me—particularly for starting and stopping!'

'Well, it looks pretty good to me!' I added. 'Milton Keynes Redways here we come!'

She put her arm around my waist and gave me a little squeeze. 'Thanks for … doing this for me, Pete. I probably would never have come if you'd told me what was in store. But I can't tell you what, … you know …'

'It was just a phone call away for me. Those Chuckle Boys did the rest!'

We all trooped into the house. Ben was paying close attention to the boys' account of how well Amy had done but more particularly about how well *they* had done in designing and implementing the whole training course.

The boys organised the biscuit barrel and brought out a bottle of elderflower cordial. They were still very excited by their great triumph and Amy's stock had risen even higher in their eyes. Then Sam was back on her lap and looking into her face. 'Can you come with us to Slieve Gallion? Please, please say you will!'

Amy looked at me. 'Slieve Gallion?'

'It's the name of our house in Normandy,' I replied. 'When we lived in Cookstown, Slieve Gallion was the name of the mountain that we could see from our kitchen.'

Annie continued, 'Years ago our parents bought two adjacent cottages in northern France which they knocked into one—this was at a time when you could get property in France for tuppence. They did a fantastic job renovating it! Pete and I spent every summer there throughout our childhood.'

Ben took over, 'You'll love it, Amy. Old oak beams, big garden, …'

'Orchard!' interrupted Sam.

'And the river running through it,' added Harry.

64

'Yea,' said Sam, 'and we have a boat race on the river every year!'

'A boat race?' smiled Amy. 'Impressive. Must be some river!'

I laughed. 'When you say *river*—ten centimetres deep at its deepest; just one splash and you've stepped across it …'

'… and when you say *boat,*' added Annie, 'think something like the length of a banana!'

'And we paint them,' added Sam excitedly. 'We hold the regatta every year!'

'Sounds great,' added Amy. She looked away and said quietly, 'You guys are … so lucky!'

'So, can you come then?' Sam wouldn't let this one go.

'Well, I don't know. It sounds so nice, but …'

'…but nothing,' I interrupted. 'I'm going to be bossy now. Look boys, I promise that if we can, Amy and I will join you for a week during the holidays!'

'Well, the school holidays start next week. We're actually heading there in a fortnight's time,' said Ben.

Annie smiled at Amy. 'What do you think, Amy? We'd really love to have you both. We'll be there for two weeks, so just come when you can and stay as long as you like—there's plenty of room.'

'And the bikes, mum. Tell her about the bikes!' said Harry excitedly.

'Oh yes, the bikes. Our family have always been big bikers—well, mum and dad used to be. And each time a bike was replaced at home, the old one went over to Slieve Gallion to live in the garage. So there's quite a handy collection there, which is perfect for us.'

'Do…do your mum and dad still use it?' Amy asked.

'Not any more, sadly,' I replied. 'Their health hasn't been so good recently and, so… they just don't feel up to long trips abroad. We pay someone to look after the garden and very occasionally we let it out to holidaymakers, but mostly it's just us that use it these days.'

Annie continued. 'Their great worry is that Slieve Gallion becomes neglected. They just love it that Pete and I use it and we keep sending them photos of the boys playing in the river and cycling round the garden.'

Amy looked thoughtful. 'It all sounds like paradise. Pete, could you put the photos and movies up on the Chuckle Boys site? Then if they have a computer your mum and dad could see them whenever they liked!'

'Yes, Uncle Pete,' the boys shouted. 'Can we do that!?'

Annie jumped in. 'Yes Pete, we *should* use the website more like that. Now mum and dad don't get out much, they would love to see the boys doing fun stuff at their home from home in France!'

I nodded. 'OK guys, I'll see what I can do! You just need to send me the pics and the movies and I can do the rest!'

13

Amy sat back contentedly in her chair. 'Another lovely meal. Thanks so much Annie,'

Annie laughed. 'Oh, don't thank me. It was Ben who made the pie. I just got it out of the freezer and slammed it into the oven!'

'Sorry Ben,' Amy smiled. 'It's just that … that's not how it works in our home!'

'So, your dad isn't very domesticated then?' asked Annie.

Amy shook her head.

'What about your mum, Amy? Is she a good cook?' asked Annie, after a pause.

Amy stared at Annie for a few moments. 'She died when I was little.'

'Oh, I'm so sorry,'

'Do you remember her, Amy?' Ben asked.

Again, Amy shook her head.

As I looked more closely at Amy's face, I could see that her cheeks were now bright red. She got up from her chair and said, 'Excuse me, I've got to go to the bathroom.'

We watched her go. Then I whispered 'As you can see, she doesn't like talking about her family.'

'Really? Oh dear,' said Annie.

It was clear that Annie was dying to know more but this was not the time.

Amy came back from the bathroom and returned to her seat. We could all see that she'd been crying. Eventually I broke the silence.

'I do hope we can get to Slieve Gallion this year, Annie.'

'The wains love having you there…will love having you both there. Let me show you some photos, Amy.'

They went through the book of snaps together. Amy remained fairly silent, as she did for the rest of the evening.

Amy and I climbed into bed. I could see that she was still rather thoughtful and subdued. 'Everything alright in Carpenter mansions?' I asked, cautiously. Amy nodded and managed a modest smile. 'Oh yes, fine thanks,' she replied. 'I've just got, you know, a bit of a headache.'

'You had a little moment, though…just after dinner. I hope everyone asking about your family hasn't upset you.'

'No, it's OK,' she replied. 'I think it's just…' Amy paused for a very long time. 'My home life's been nothing like what you've been used to, Pete. Being here with a normal family has been…it's been a bit of a shock. Everyone's so…involved in each other's life and so caring. I think it just hit me how different my life has been to yours.'

I paused to let her say more but nothing was forthcoming.

'Would you prefer not to go to Slieve Gallion?' I asked.

'No! I *do* want to go!' said Amy, with a sudden intensity. 'I would love to go. It's just…'

'…what *did* happen to your mum, Aims?'

She shook her head. 'Only dad knows.'

'Have you asked him?'

'He's not good with questions.'

'Not good?'

'She was French, I think.'

Amy put a hand on my shoulder. 'The thing is, Pete, how can I go to France without a passport?' She looked at me for an answer. 'Remember I told you at that meal.'

'Oh yes.' I frowned trying in vain to see a way around this obstacle. 'You could apply for one, I suppose.'

'Can you get passports that quickly? In a couple of weeks?'

'No. I don't think so.'

'I don't even have a birth certificate. I guess I must have but I've never seen it.'

'If your dad had it, where would he keep it?'

'All I know is I've seen a box with a padlock that he keeps in a drawer in his bedroom. It could be in there.'

'It would be very handy to get a peep inside that box…' I said.

'I think the key's on his keyring and that stays in his pocket. But this is all just guesswork. Actually, I've no idea what he keeps in the box.'

Amy suddenly looked like a deflated balloon. 'Oh. this is useless, Pete! Everything I try to do always seems to get … what's the word?'

'Bollocksed?' I suggested helpfully.

'That's it,' replied Amy, managing a weak smile. 'Bollocksed!'

'Well,' I continued, 'You're right. We might have a bit of a problem getting you to Slieve Gallion. But, the good thing is, if I go without you…I promise to…urm…send you a postcard. Scout's honour!'

There were squawks from Amy followed by a firm punch on the arm.

'Ouch!' I cried out in mock pain.

'Shhh,' giggled Amy, 'You'll wake the wains!'

14

Amy twisted in her seat to take another look at the bicycle which we'd managed to squeeze into the back of my estate.

'I can't believe Annie gave me her old bike!'

'It's great isn't it!' I replied. 'I hope this sorts out some of your transport problems.'

'Independence! Yippee! Oh, I'm going to need a helmet, though!' Amy was experiencing a newly acquired love of the two-wheeled mode of transport.

'Is Halfords open today, I wonder?' I asked.

'Siri, *Halfords Milton Keynes opening hours Sunday*,' I said to my phone and back came the answer that it was open until five o'clock. 'Let's go straight there then!'

Amy looked slightly embarrassed.

'Hey, moneybags, this one's on me!' I said.

Amy smiled. 'You're a very nice man. And if you ever need a favour from me, you only have to ask!'

I laughed out loud because I knew, that she knew, that we were both *on a promise* that evening.

We sat in silence for a few minutes. Then Amy said, 'I really loved this weekend away. Thanks for bouncing me into it!'

After a moment, she said 'Are you actually Irish, Pete?'

'Yes!'

'From where?'

'Well, do you want the long version or the short version?'

'Oh, the long version please. I'm in no rush!'

'OK then, you've asked for it! The Campbells were originally from the west coast of Scotland. We came across in the 16 hundreds and settled in the nearest county of Northern Ireland, which was …'

I adopted the tone of a strict schoolteacher testing the class, 'Yes, Miss Carpenter?'

'Galway, sir,' she replied smartly. 'I'd say it was county Galway, sir!'

'Not even close, Miss Carpenter! That's on the west coast, unfortunately. The answer I was looking for was Antrim. But you get a house point for knowing the name of an Irish county.'

'Ooh, thank you sir,' she replied in a rather elaborately coquettish manner. 'I've always wanted one of those! But why did your ancestors leave Scotland, do you think?'

'Well, that was the time of the *Plantation of Ulster*, when the English rulers tried to quell the 'revolting Irish' by giving their land away to people who they could count on to be loyal to the crown.'

'But to the Scottish?' Amy questioned. 'Since when were the Scottish loyal to the English?'

'Well, quite!' I replied. 'There was also a suggestion of cattle-rustling by clan Campbell and clan Graham so it may be that we were all shipped out of Scotland just to get rid of us. Who knows, really!'

'So did the family stay in Antrim?'

'All I know is that at some point we moved further inland to County Tyrone ... to a great little place called Cookstown, where Annie and I spent our early years.'

'Really?' Amy said in surprise. 'I can't exactly detect an accent.'

'Not from me—I was only four when we came across, but you can still hear it a bit when Annie has drink taken. She was seven and she hasn't entirely lost it. There are still some words she says, like *yer man* ...'

'And *wains*!' laughed Amy. 'I've worked out that means kids?'

'It's actually short for 'wee ones'!'

Amy nodded. 'Oh, yes, that makes sense! So, what about your mum and dad? What brought them to England?'

'Both teachers,' I replied. 'Dad was head of a small primary school in the middle of nowhere outside Cookstown. Mum's background was in science teaching—secondary. They both managed to get a job in the Midlands.'

'But why did they want to leave lovely Cookstown?'

'I think it was the Troubles. Things were pretty tense over there throughout the 90s and they didn't want Annie and me to get caught up in it all. They were lucky—they both got nice teaching jobs in Leamington Spa, which is where Annie and I were brought up. We loved it there.'

'So, with the long holidays, your family were able to spend a good amount of time in the French house. Is that why your French is so … groovy?'

I laughed. 'Not nearly as groovy as yours! But, the thing is, no one in that part of Normandy speaks much English so we all had to learn the lingo. I know enough to get by!'

As it so often does on the homeward part of the journey, the time just flew past. We got to Halfords in plenty of time for Amy to acquire her helmet and bike chain lock. We also popped into Tescos and stocked up with food for an evening meal before driving back to my flat.

Over a coffee, we got out our music playlists and began comparing favourites. After dinner, I placed the dishes into the dishwasher and I put on the kettle for a coffee.

'Well that was nice,' said Amy. 'So, what shall we do now?'

'Hmm,' I replied. 'Sunday night—I don't think there's anything very much on the telly.'

'No, not on a Sunday night.'

'We could play something. Do you play … table tennis?' I asked.

'Table tennis? Do you have all the, you know, the gear for that?'

'No!' I replied.

There was a pause.

'I see,' said Amy.

'Well,' I continued, 'it's been quite a busy couple of days.'

Amy nodded, 'It certainly has!'

'I don't know about you,' I continued, 'but I could really do with … an early night.'

Amy gave an exaggerated yawn. 'Yea, me too …'

Suddenly I made a dash for the stairs with Amy in hot pursuit. Half-way up she grabbed my leg, quickly clambered over the top of me and within two seconds had disappeared into the bedroom. She was already lying languidly on the bed when I followed her in.

She gave me a cheeky grin. 'Too slow, old man. Surely you know it's bad form to keep a lady waiting?'

15

Amy had reluctantly come to the conclusion that she wasn't quite ready for taking her bicycle onto the public highway. So, over the next week we returned each lunchtime to my flat where she could put in some practice around the largely deserted Fishermead estate. It was the following Monday when she decided to bite the bullet, abandon the bus and cycle home after work.

'I wish you could just stay here,' I said to her as she strapped on her helmet.

Amy looked tearful. 'Me too,' she said, 'but you know I have to go. Somebody'll be wanting their supper, won't they!'

I nodded. 'Yep. That's what we agreed. We need to do this bit with our heads, not our hearts. She climbed onto Annie's old bike and slowly pedalled off in the direction of the Redway. As I waved her off, I couldn't help thinking about what sort of a reception she might receive from the old bastard when she arrived home with her new bike and accessories. I was consoled by the thought that fortunately, these days, Amy had become very skilled at lying!

I went back into my flat and treated myself to a pre-prandial glass of wine. I thought back to how my life had been transformed in just a couple of months. B.A.—that's Before Amy—my world was calm, well-ordered and free from any real meaningful emotional turmoil. But actually, it was also isolated, repetitive and boring. Whatever else I felt about being with her, she certainly made me feel alive! The shame was that the time we could spend together was so very limited. The control exercised by her dad on her movements meant that spending evenings and weekends together seemed out of reach. Perhaps I should ask her to move in with me? Mmm…it was a very attractive thought but would she want to? Was it too early in the relationship? Also, in fairness I needed to actually break up with Clare first before inviting my new girlfriend to move in! I resolved to park the thought for a few weeks until I was sure that all these factors were in place.

Next morning I went to my office earlier than usual. Amy was already there. I looked over to give her a morning greeting but I could see that all was not well. Her eyes were red and puffy and she didn't seem able to return my encouraging smile. I went over to her desk and said 'Could you just pop round to my office, Amy?' She nodded, but clearly with a heavy heart.

A minute later she was in my office and sobbing in my arms.

'What's up, Amy? Has he been horrible to you?'

She nodded, wordlessly.

'So ... what was his problem this time?'

Amy took a couple of deep breaths and then sat down beside my desk.

'Well, it all started with the bike. Where did you get that? I explained that it was a gift but that seemed to make it worse. So, which of your *many* friends would give *you* a bike. Then he saw the new helmet and security lock and he really hit the roof. Those things are expensive. We're not made of money! You've been lying to me. How long has this been going on? On and on it went—accusations, put-downs, anger, it was relentless!'

'So, what did you say to him?'

Amy paused before answering. 'Nothing at first. I just let him rant away in his usual, bullying manner. But then...I did something I've never done with him before.'

I raised my eyebrows.

'I snapped! I suddenly found myself shouting and screaming back and...I told him some home truths that I should have said long ago!'

'Such as?'

During this whole conversation, Amy's voice had begun to increase steadily in volume. By now the decibel level had increased from normal conversational to distinctly and, for her, uncharacteristically loud.

'I said to him, how bloody dare you lecture me about money…'

'Really?'

'…particularly when I'm the one who pays for everything in this house…why should you be the one who makes all the decisions? And then, I'm afraid, I called him a bad word!'

'Oh? And what was that?'

'I said he was a controlling…you know?'

'Erm… nope! A controlling…?'

'Rhymes with…Tommy Tucker!'

'Gosh! Well, that was telling him. Well done you! So, you really…lost your shit!'

Amy covered her face with her hands and began to sob. 'Oh Pete. I can't tell you. It was just…horrendous!'

At that moment the door opened and Stacey stuck her head in. 'Hi guys. Just checking in. Everything all right here?'

I waved her in. She closed the door behind her and sat down beside us. Amy was still sitting with her hands covering her face. Stacey put an arm around Amy's shoulder. 'You just let it out, girl!' she said comfortingly. Amy turned to her and shook her head. 'Sorry, Stacey. I can't talk about it just now. I need to go to the bathroom.' She stood up picked up her handbag and headed down the corridor.

While she was away I did my best to fill Stacey in with what was going on. She was appalled. 'Poor girl, poor girl,' she repeated. 'What a right old so-and-so that man is!'

Five minutes later, Amy returned in a slightly better state than when she had left with her hair brushed and the tears on her face washed off. She did her best to give Stacey a cheerful smile. 'Sorry, Stacey. I'm just…all over the place!'

As I had hoped, Stacey immediately rallied to her cause. 'Listen, Amy, Pete's filled me in on the basics of what's been happening. With all you're going through, there's no way you can be thinking about work. I want you to take three days sick leave as from now and I'll sort out the paperwork.'

A look of intense relief swept over Amy's face and she didn't make any attempt to protest at the suggestion. 'Thanks so much, Stacey,' I said with genuine gratitude. She smiled at me, 'I think I'm leaving her in safe hands!' Then she turned back to Amy. 'Just be kind to yourself, Amy. You'll get through it!' She got up and made her way back to her office.

I turned back to Amy who by now was starting to look a little more like her old self again. I thought back to my deliberations from the night before about choosing the ideal occasion for Amy to move in with me. But different times call for different measures.

'Now Amy. I'd like to say something about your living arrangements. You know you can't go back there with your dad.' She stared at me with a confused expression but said nothing.

'So,' I continued, 'I would love it if you would…move in with me, as from today!' Again, Amy didn't move and continued to stare at me. Her face bore no expression that I could discern. Suddenly she got out of her chair and threw her arms around my neck and squeezed me 'til it hurt.

'I'm taking that as a yes, then!' I managed to blurt out.

We drove back to my flat and could see that she looked totally washed out. Amy hadn't slept at all the previous night and so after a cup of tea, she took herself off to sleep in my bedroom. I woke her at midday with a bowl of soup and a cheese roll. Over lunch we were able to have a calmer conversation to consider what lay ahead.

'I still can't believe this, Pete. Everything that's happened in the last 24 hours is just…a blur!'

I grinned at her. 'But I'm really excited. Now we can spend evenings together, weekends together, go away together if we want. We're answerable to nobody!'

She nodded. 'I know. It's what I've secretly wanted for a while. I just couldn't see how to make it happen. One thing though. I've only got the clothes I stand up in. I'm going to have to go back home and collect my things.'

I looked at my watch. 'Do you happen to know what time yer man leaves the house in the morning and when he gets back?'

Amy frowned. 'I can't be sure since I'm out all day myself. But I'd say he always goes off in his van in the mornings. Sometimes he's there when I get home and sometimes he's not. But we just need to look out for his blue van. No van, no dad!'

'In that case,' I replied, 'we need to get going. Let's get in, load up the car with everything you want to keep and bring your stuff back here. Just one thing—that box that your dad keeps in his bedroom drawer. I'd really like to see what's in there. Who knows—maybe we'll find your birth certificate.'

I went to my clock repair cupboard and lifted out my bag of tricks. Then I unzipped a side pocket and removed my favourite little gadget.

'What the heck is that?' Amy asked.

'Let me introduce my Lock Cowboy. Sometimes the clocks that Marta gives me are locked—they never come with a key, of course. With the help of this little beast, more often than not, I can open them up. I'm going to give your dad's padlock a go with it.'

'Oh God, Pete, please be careful,' Amy said nervously. 'If he finds out that his box has been jemmied he'll just…he'll just go berserk!'

'Don't worry. I'll be careful. It probably won't work anyway but…but you'd never know.'

'Are we really doing this Pete?'

I kissed her on the forehead. 'Yup, we really are. Let's giddyup cowboy!'

16

Amy directed me to her home, in a small, rather 'unloved' estate in the outskirts of Bletchley. I was aware that the surrounding streets had more than their share of abandoned urban detritus—a wheel-less car perched on bricks as well as scatterings of litter and broken bicycle parts. From my previous visits I had always picked her up from the Greggs corner shop so I'd never actually seen her flat. She pointed it out and we drove slowly past it.

'Great, no van!' said Amy.

'So, no dad!' I replied.

I reversed the car up onto the hard standing at the front of the flat and we both got out. The curtains were still closed. They were made of flimsy 1950s lace, so ancient that they were now very faded and yellowing. The exterior had the look of the sort of sad accommodation that I remembered from my student days in Manchester. Amy took her keys from her handbag, opened the door and stepped inside. I followed her but paused at the open doorway to take in their interior living space. In one corner was an old portable TV. Facing it was a battered ancient armchair, the springs of which had seen better days. A tiny tablecloth covered a small card table which was placed against the wall under the front window. Beside it were two wooden chairs that had clearly learned a few life lessons from the school of hard knocks. The kitchen area was an extension of the living room; it contained just a sink, a cooker and two open shelves with a couple of pots and a frying pan handle sticking out. On the adjacent wall was a third smaller shelf that contained only cans of Carling lager—two unopened 24-packs and three or four loose cans. Leading from the main room were three internal doors, which I presumed gave access to two bedrooms and a bathroom.

Amy pointed to the little card table. 'Just sit there, Pete; I'll do this,' she whispered. She went into the kitchen area, opened a drawer and removed a couple of black liner bags.

'I'll go and get my clothes,' she said, opening one of the internal doors. 'Oh, hang on…' She went into the second bedroom and came back with a padlocked metal box which she placed on the table before me. 'See what you can do with this, Pete. But please, please be careful!'

I smiled encouragingly at her.

'I will!' I whispered back. 'But don't hold your breath. This heist is all slightly above the pay grade of Mister Lock Cowboy! But he says he'll give it a go!'

Ten minutes later, Amy plonked two filled liner bags on the floor beside me and sat down on the other wooden chair. She still had a worried look.

'So, how's the lock-cracking going, Pete?'

'Why are we whispering?' I replied with a smile.

'Oh, this place! Walls have ears!' she replied in an even more nervous voice.

'Well, no luck so far! But I haven't quite given up.'

Amy glanced at her watch. 'I think we have to be going, though, Pete. He could be back at any time…'

'Just give me five more minutes!'

'OK,' she replied anxiously. 'Just five more…and then we really need to, you know, make a move!'

In the event we didn't have to wait five more minutes. After two minutes the lock suddenly went 'Click!' and sprang open.

'I've bloody done it,' I shouted.

'Shh!' was Amy's immediate response, as she grabbed my arm. 'You're a very clever boy!'

I opened the lid and looked inside. It was a mess of papers and documents. I glanced at one. 'Well, that might be your birth certificate, Amy—or it might not. But whatever it is, I think we've uncovered a treasure trove here! Can you find me a bag?'

Amy went back into the kitchen area, pulled out a plastic shopping bag from the drawer and brought it over to me.

'Let's just take the lot for now,' I said as I scooped everything into the Tesco bag. We can go through it properly when we get back.' Amy deftly shut the lid of the box, snapped the padlock shut and returned the box to her father's bedroom drawer. I looked down at the two liner bags on the floor. 'Is that all you're taking?'

'Yes,' she nodded. 'That's everything I own. Over the years I've learned to travel light!' Suddenly I had a thought. 'Aims, your books? You haven't packed them!'

Amy smiled. 'Books?' Amy pointed to her laptop computer. 'Don't panic! They're all inside that little magic box! Let's go!'

We set off on the fifteen-minute drive back to my flat. As I manoeuvred the narrow roads to exit Amy's estate I made a mental note—I must now remember to call it *our* flat, not *my* flat. Looking across I could see that Amy was lost inside a world that I knew nothing of so I decided not to intrude. After ten minutes or so, curiosity got the better of her. She picked up the Tesco bag lying at her feet and placed it on her lap. She couldn't resist taking some of the contents out and leafing through them. Suddenly she let out an ear-piercing shriek.

'My God, Amy. What the …'

'My passport!' she shouted. 'I've just found my passport … the passport that I … that I never had!'

'You're kidding! Is the photo up-to-date?'

'It is! And I'm checking the dates. Yes, it's valid for … another eight years! Weirdly, the envelope is addressed to me at dad's address so … he must have applied for it pretending to be me and then intercepted it.'

'That's so brilliant, though, Amy. But how the hell did he…?'

Amy was already one step ahead. 'The *issued on* date is around the time I got my job at the university. He said then that I needed to have a proper photo taken for getting the job … which was actually true.'

'… and the sneaky bugger used a spare copy to send off a passport application in your name without saying a word.'

Amy fell silent for a moment. 'What I don't get is … why would he do that…?' I considered the question. 'No,' I said slowly. 'Neither do I.'

When we got back, I carried the two liner bags of Amy's possessions inside and placed them on the floor of my—sorry, *our*—bedroom. Amy brought in the Tesco bag of precious documents and papers and placed in on the kitchen table. To my great surprise, even after we had made and drunk a cup of tea, the bag remained there undisturbed. Amy was sitting silently looking very drawn and unhappy. I pointed to the bag. 'Hey, Aims, aren't you, you know, going to have a peep inside?' But answer came there none. Eventually she managed to recover her powers of speech. 'It's all too much, Pete. I just can't, you know…'

I could only imagine what an emotional upheaval she'd just gone through. It wasn't only that she'd walked away from her home but she had also walked away from the one person who had been her constant companion for the entirety of her life. I took her hands in mine. 'Talk to me,' I said, eventually. 'Tell me what thoughts are buzzing round that brain of yours!'

After a long pause, she said 'I'm thinking…how the hell is he going to manage on his own?'

'What do you mean,' I asked.

'Well,' she continued, 'as you know, I pay the rent, I pay the bills. He hasn't actually got any money at all. I don't think he can survive on his own!'

I really wasn't prepared to accept this version of reality without putting in my tuppence worth. 'Amy, first of all, you're 23, you earn your own money and you've a right to be independent. But setting that aside, let's look at your dad. He isn't as lacking in funds as you think.' Amy's eyes widened.

'For a start,' I continued, 'I noticed there were a lot of cans of lager in your kitchen. Did *you* buy those?' Amy shook her head. 'No,' I continued, 'I bet *he* did!'

'And what about the van? He does a lot of driving. Running a vehicle is expensive. Who pays for the petrol, the tax, the insurance, the repairs, the annual MOT test?'

'Well, yes, he does,' Amy said slowly.

'The truth is, Amy, your dad *does* have money— you know he has some mystery driving job but he's a bit shy about telling you how much he earns from it. Anyway, he's not a helpless child! He's fit and healthy, for God's sake! If he needs more, he can try to get a different job or if he's really strapped he can apply for universal credit from the government.'

Amy drew in a long deep breath. Then she nodded. 'I s'pose' she said eventually. 'But I still can't look inside the bag.'

'Why not?'

'Well, I just don't know what I'm going to find. And on top of all that there must be a lot of dad's papers there too—maybe his driving licence and passport and things like that. I need to get them back to him.'

I nodded. 'Would it help if I took a quick whizz through the bag and pulled out the bits and pieces that are clearly his.

'Thanks Pete,' she replied tearfully. 'That would be a real help.'

'So then I could stick them in an envelope and push them through his door,' I continued.

'No...' At this moment, Amy began to sob. '...the biggest thing of all, Pete, is... I've never actually told him I was leaving. I just slipped out like a ...thief in the night. That was a horrible thing to do!'

Up until this point, Amy had been just about holding her emotions in check. Suddenly the dam burst and she started sobbing, and sobbing. I put my arms around her and tried my best to comfort her.'

'Tring, Tring,' went the doorbell.

'Who the hell could that be,' I mused aloud. 'I'm not answering it.'

'Tring, Tring,' it went again. I still didn't move. 'Tring, Tring, Tring,' it went for a third time but now more insistent.

'I'll get rid of them,' I said and got up from the sofa to open the door.

'Pete hun. Surprise!'

'Clare! Jesus! What the hell are you doing here?'

17

Clare made a face. 'Well, Pete, what kinda welcome is that? Isn't it a nice surprise?'

I just stared at her.

'Baby, I'm bursting for a pee. Let me in will you, I'm dying here.' She crossed her legs dramatically.

I pulled open the door to let her in. She stepped around two massive suitcases and walked rapidly across the threshold. 'The bathroom's at the top of the stairs.'

I looked across at Amy who was still sitting on the sofa, her face streaked with tears and by now looking down at her feet. I went across to her and whispered 'She had to use the bathroom. I promise I'll get rid of her asap.'

I stood awkwardly waiting for Clare to reappear.

After five very long minutes, we heard the toilet flush and Clare came back downstairs with her baseball cap in one hand and her coat over her arm.

'I've just seen what I look like in the mirror. Geez, I'm dying to have a shower.'

She looked over at Amy who was still in a dishevelled heap. 'Hi, I'm Clare.'

'Clare, this is Amy.'

Clare looked at Amy, then back to me and then looked at Amy once more.

'So…how did you find me anyway, Clare?'

'All I have is your mother's number. I rang her and as usual I couldn't understand a word she was saying. She had to spell it out to the cab driver.' Then pointing to the front door, she said 'Oh Pete, my luggage. Carry my bags in for me will you. They weigh an absolute ton!'

I didn't move.

'Is there a problem, hun?'

'Yes Clare, there is a problem. I'm wondering why you've just turned up like this out of the blue when I haven't heard a thing from you in months?'

She pondered the question carefully. 'Well, Pete, I'm as free as a bird, now. You remember Donna? What a loser she turned out to be. She became impossible. No integrity. I just can't operate with people who lack integrity…'

'Did you get the sack, then, is that it?' I asked.

She responded with a half smile and turned slowly to face Amy. 'So…Jamie…who are you again, sweetie?'

Amy stared back at her silently.

I answered for her. 'Amy's my girlfriend…and she lives here with me.'

'Girlfriend?' She looked back at me in distain. 'Swapped me for a newer model, huh? Boy, did I get that one wrong?'

'Look Clare, you can't stay here tonight, if that's what you were thinking. You either phone a friend or find a hotel somewhere.'

She fixed me with a hard stare. 'So…did we break up, Pete? I don't remember us having that conversation.'

'Clare, I can count on one hand the conversations we've had over the last 12 months! You wanted to build a new life back in America and I told you at the time that was not for me.'

Clare's face flushed. 'Well, you never even tried! My parents loved you. They took you here, there and everywhere but you couldn't wait to get back…to *this?*' She swung her arms around with an expression of disgust. 'But don't you worry about me, Pete. I've got friends, places I can go. I lived in…this…goddam country for twelve years, so that's not a problem.'

'Well, that's good then. So…'

'…and by the way, Pete,' she interrupted, 'for your information, no, I did *not* get the sack. '

Clare suddenly looked like she was going to sob. 'I came back because…I wanted to start a…new chapter in my life.'

'What chapter?'

'I am desperate to have…a baby and I wanted…you…to be the father.'

'Jesus Christ, Clare! Seriously?'

Her eyes flashed in anger. 'Maybe you haven't noticed, Pete, but I'm 37 years of age and I'm running out of time. It's all right for you. Your biological clock isn't ticking. It's different for women!'

I looked across at Amy and saw that she had sunk even lower into the sofa. I shook my head slowly. 'I don't buy it. When did these "maternal feelings" come on. You certainly never thought to share them with me.'

'That was meant to be a surprise, you dummy!' she shouted angrily. 'That's why I'm here, bozo!'

I took a long look at Clare. I understood her well enough to recognise her gift for improvisation. This pantomime had to stop.

'I don't actually believe any of this!'

She looked at me with fury. 'You're an unfeeling bastard Peter Campbell and I wouldn't have your goddam baby if you were the last goddam man on planet Earth!'

'Well, those maternal feelings seem to have been short-lived, then! I think it's time you left, Clare.'

Clare stared at me in amazement. In all the many years we'd been together, she'd never seen me stand up to her in this way. She suddenly changed tack and instantly adopted a more conciliatory tone. 'Look Pete, hun, I didn't come here to have a row with you. Let's all just rewind. I think…you and I…we just need to catch up calmly. We've got a lot of things we need to sort out…'

'…like what?'

'Oh, lots of stuff, but not like this. Let's just get together over lunch, we'll grab a sandwich and talk sensibly. Let's do it tomorrow—OK?'

'I'm in Cambridge all day tomorrow. It's not going to work Clare…'

'Tell you what, Pete, I'll just give…what's her name…Stacey a buzz. She always knew your diary better than you did. We'll fix something up. I know, we could go to that nice Thai restaurant in the city centre. I liked that place!'

'Anyway,' she said, shooting a glance across at a very miserable looking Amy, 'I can see this isn't the best time for a social visit so…I'll shoot off.'

She grabbed her handbag and fished out her phone. No one spoke as she started dialling.

'Hi, I need an Uber to Milton Keynes station. What? Oh!'

She turned to me. 'Where the hell am I, Pete?'

'74, Turner's Croft, Flat 1.'

'It's Flat 1, seventy…what?'

'Seventy four, Turner's Croft.' I repeated louder.

'Seventy four, Turner's Croft. Jesus! What, ten minutes? Try and make it soon…! Oh, he's gone.'

She threw the phone into her bag and started pulling on her coat and zipping it up. Anyway, I've got my luggage to sit on—if they're still there in this "cozy" little neighbourhood.'

'Bye Pete. Bye…erm Jamie.' I'll be in touch, Pete. She opened the front door, walked out and banged it "firmly" behind her. Neither Amy nor I moved or spoke for a while. We just listened. Eventually, Amy whispered 'What if the taxi doesn't come?'

'Oh, it will, it will. It better had!'

We held our breath every time a car drove past.

Then we heard a car pull up. Moments later, all trace of Clare had vanished and I could breathe again.

18

Amy and I just sat together holding hands in silence. As I thought of Clare setting off for God-knows-where with those two ridiculous suitcases, I found myself retreating into the music library of my mind. What was playing there today, I wondered?

It turned out to be a song that has long given me the shivers—Astrud Gilberto singing, *How Insensitive.*

Why, he must have asked
Could I just turn and stare in icy silence
What was I to do
What can one do
When a love affair is over ... over.

I started to fight back the tears that were welling up. I jumped out of my chair and, switching on the kettle said, 'Well, I don't know about you, Aims, but I could do with a cup of tea!'

But Amy was still sitting looking totally shell-shocked. 'That was ... that was really horrible!' she said eventually.

I could see that she too was on the verge of tears. I went over to where she was sitting and she put her arms around my waist. The silence was broken only by the click of the kettle to *Off*...but neither of us moved. Then, to my great surprise, I found myself starting to sob gently. Amy hugged me tighter and rubbed my back with her hand.

'Poor you, Pete. That can't have been easy.'

I nodded weakly. Eventually I was able to speak.

'You see, I've always been the special person who could fix it for her. However big the problem, she always believed that I could

… make it go away. But not this time. This is one she'll have to fix herself.'

Amy patted my back gently. 'I'm sorry, Pete. I'm so sorry!'

I went over to the kettle and switched it on again. Amy found a packet of Hobnobs in the kitchen cupboard and we treated ourselves to a soothing hot drink and a sugar boost. After a few moments of thoughtful silence, Amy said, 'Pete, can I ask you about something Clare said. She seems to be all set for a big meet-up with you over the next few days. Do you think…'

'…Amy, believe me, that is not happening!' I interrupted. 'All that talk was just…talk.'

'But she said she was going to do a diary check with Stacey to fix a date.'

'Well, for a start, she won't. But even if she does, I'll be telling Stacey to keep it vague. Seriously, Aims, I have no plans to meet up with Clare at all and when she's thought it through herself, she'll come to the same conclusion!'

Amy nodded. Then she said softly 'Pete, now…something else…please don't be mad but…I've just made a decision. I need…I need to go back.'

'To your dad's?' I asked incredulously. 'But Aims, you've only just moved in here!'

'No, no, I'm not *moving* back there! It's just, I need to say…to say goodbye. I owe him that.'

'Well, that's a matter of opinion…'

'…He's my dad, Pete. He may be…flawed, but at the end of the day he's still my dad.'

'I don't want you to go, Amy!'

She looked at me and said nothing. Eventually she said simply, 'I have to!' I could see that her mind was made up.

I sighed. 'Well, if that's what you really want, Aims, I'll not stand in your way.'

She stood up. 'I'll get my coat from the bedroom, then.'

'What? You're going *now*?'

'Yup, he'll be wondering where I am otherwise.'

'Blimey! OK then—shall I pull out his passport and any other important papers of his so you can bring them with you?'

'Thanks, Pete. Let me just do this.'

While Amy was upstairs, I had a quick shufty through the plastic bag. I managed to pull out her dad's passport, driving licence and birth certificate and put them into an envelope. If there turned out to be other key documents of his in the bag, we could always send them on later. She returned to the living room wearing her coat. I handed her the envelope and picked up my car keys.

'OK, Aims, let's go. I can wait in the car 'til you're done.' Amy shook her head. 'Thanks Pete but I really need to do this one on my own. Don't worry. I know the bus route and the bus timetable so getting there and back isn't a problem.' She kissed my cheek. 'I just want us to make a fresh start and not have this thing hanging over me.'

I looked at her askance. 'Are you really sure?'

'I'm really sure!' She checked that her old house keys were still in her pocket. 'If he's not back, I'll just let myself in and wait for him. I don't know how long this thing will take but when it's done, it'll be done!'

I watched disconsolately as she exited the door, pulling it gently shut behind her. At least she didn't slam it like my former girlfriend had just done 30 minutes before.

The more I thought about this outing of Amy's the less I liked it. Travelling by bus in the early evening and returning God knows when at night seemed to me to be a much less safe option that using the car. Also, could she really trust this man to maintain his temper when she shared with him the bad news that she'd left for good. On top of everything else, she would have to come clean that she had broken into his secret document box and made off with his most valued possessions. If her dad had a violent streak, this might just be the trigger for it to come to the surface.

But then on the other hand...Amy was an adult and I needed to give her the freedom to act independently. I had no intention to turn into a younger version of her controlling dad. In the end I had no choice but just to sit tight, let her get on with it and do the one thing I could do in the circumstances. Worry!

I spent the next two hours busily trying to occupy my mind. I sat down at my computer, opened the much-visited file Pete's Thesis and started to re-read the latest chapter that I'd been working on. After five minutes, I found myself thinking, "Why the hell am I doing this? What a ridiculous idea!" I'd really bombed out on that one and closed down the file. Then I got out an old cryptic crossword book and had a look at the most recent puzzle that I'd last attempted B.A. (Before Amy). Three clues were still unsolved. Hmm, well, I quickly discovered that if I'd been unable to solve these three clues a couple of months ago, then as sure as hell I couldn't solve them now.

I knew that Amy was likely to be hungry when she got back, as indeed would I. I had a rootle around the freezer and uncovered a leek and potato pie that I'd made weeks before but forgotten all about. I pulled it out, popped it into the microwave and set it to defrost.

So, what now? The one standby in these sorts of situations was my guitar. I still had the Astrud Gilberto song running around my head so I checked out the chords from the Ultimate-Guitar website and gave it a go. Success. The chords were fab and I'd finally found a task that I could stick at for the rest of the evening.

I was still cradling my guitar when, at around 8.15, there was a gentle tapping with a fingernail on the window. I rushed to open the door and Amy stepped forward to give me a much-appreciated hug and kiss. I stepped back and took a good look at her. Yup—totally washed out and exhausted.

'Oh, Pete,' was all she could say, shaking her head.

'I'm just relieved you're still alive!' I said, kissing her again. 'Talk about entering the lion's den, Amy! My mind's been racing thinking about what he could have done to you.' Amy just looked at me intently but said nothing.

I walked over to the microwave oven and switched it on. Then I laid the table, poured us a drink and in no time, we were sitting down to a much-appreciated meal.

'Well?' I asked, eventually.

'Well, it could have been worse, I suppose,' she replied. 'There was a bit of shouting at first. The breaking-and-entering of his strong box was a real low point. He went mad about that part!'

'Well, I'm not surprised at that...'

'...but at least I was able to hand over his most valuable documents so that was something. But eventually, when he'd calmed down a bit, I got to say it. I told him that I was leaving— well that I had actually left—and why I'd done it. And I also told him about you.'

'And did he accept it?'

'I think he could see he had to. Particularly after the way I'd stood up to him last night; there was much less...bluster. I wasn't asking permission—I was telling him what I intended to do...and there was nothing else to say.'

'Gosh! She who must be obeyed!' I said. 'You're turning into a right little Miss Bossy Boots!' We both laughed at that because this particular personality type seemed so very far removed from Amy's usual gentle style.

'So, any plans to...you know...keep in touch, now that you've moved out?'

Amy shook her head. 'No, nothing like that. It wasn't discussed. I just said an awkward goodbye, handed him my flat key and headed out the door.'

'And...any regrets?'

She smiled. 'No, this is my life now and it just feels so...right!'

'You must be knackered, though,' I continued. She nodded. 'Yes. You might have to carry me up!'

'Fireman's lift OK for you?'

'Thanks, Fireman Sam. That would be a lovely treat. But no bottom slapping on the way up the stairs, if you please!'

'I assure you Ms Carpenter, your bottom will be safe in my hands!'

Amy smiled. 'Ha! Yea, that's exactly what I'm talking about! One thing though, Pete. I wouldn't mind a quick peep inside the Tesco bag before I go up. I'd really like to find my birth certificate. I can take a more thorough look tomorrow while you're in Cambridge.'

I smiled. 'I think I saw it! But there's only one way to find out!'

19

We emptied out the contents of the bag onto the table and Amy quickly shuffled through them. Her eye was soon drawn to a small envelope marked 'Amy's Birth Certificate'.

She pulled out the contents and opened it on the table. I watched as she quietly mouthed the words, *acte de naissance*. 'Pete,' she choked in disbelief. 'I don't have a birth certificate. I have an *acte de naissance*. My birth certificate... is in French!'

I moved over to sit next to her. It was unbelievable. Amy was born in France and now had official papers to show that she almost certainly had French nationality.

She carefully went through the document line by line.

Date et lieu de naissance
'I was born on the 14th of June, 2001. Well at least that's right. Place of birth was Honfleur.'

'Honfleur!' I exclaimed. 'We go there all the time. It's only about an hour's drive from Slieve Gallion!'

Amy closed her eyes and let out a mighty silent scream.

'Next comes NOM.
'My name is ... my name is ... Aimée Clotilde Charpentier.'
'Pete, look at that spelling of Aimée. That's the real spelling of my name. And Clotilde is my middle name. I love that name! And my surname is ... oh my God! Not Carpenter! It's Charpentier, which is French for Carpenter!'

I gave her a quick hug. 'Keep going!'

'OK next, *Prenom(s) et nom du père*.

94

That's given as Maurice Charles. Well, that's right! And his surname is … JOHNS. What?? I've never heard him use that name. His name is Maurice JOHN. There's no 's' What is going on, Pete? None of this makes sense.'

Amy continued. 'Next are my mother's names. She is Élise Camille Charpentier. Charpentier? I just knew it! … As I've always suspected, I've been named after my mother all along!'

'God!' I interjected. 'But how could that have happened … in France of all places?'

'I wonder,' she replied, 'if my dad was actually not there at the signing of the documents. Otherwise, I doubt if he would have ever agreed to me being given my mother's name but maybe she just took matters into her own hands.'

By now, Amy had gone into a total trance. 'Élise Camille'. Aren't those the most beautiful names you've ever heard!'

Then I pointed to the last line on the card. It read,
Le cas échéant, date et lieu de la reconnaissance.

'Can you translate that, Amy?'

'Um, it means, 'If known, the date and place of … recognition'. I don't know what that means, though.'

'I see they've put down Lisieux for that,' I added. 'That's even closer to Slieve Gallion!'

We sat in total silence for 30 seconds, taking in what we had just read.

'My God, Amy. This is massive!'

'You bet!'

'Amy, we could use a bit of help with this document. We need to talk to a French national who can unpick it for you.'

Amy nodded slowly. 'And do you know such a person?'

I thought about it for a moment. 'Not really, but I think I know someone who…might know someone!'

Ping! 'Oh, that's me!' I picked up my phone. 'My God, it's mum. I just thought she might get in touch today!' Amy tidied up the papers that she'd been looking at and settled back to listen in.

'Hi mum, how's things? Glad to see you've finally mastered FaceTime!'

'Oh Peter. No, well I think I know what I'm doin' this time. Sure, isn't it great to be lookin' at your lovely face!'

'Well, I'd like to be seeing your lovely face too, mum but all I can see is your arm.'

'Oh, is that better?'

'No. Now I've got a perfect view of the piano. Just look at the screen mum. If you're looking straight at me, I'll be looking straight at you. That's better. That's great. So... anything strange or startling to report, then?'

'Ow, not much. But, well, now you come to say, there was one thing I just wanted... I got such a funny call from that Clare. I thought she'd gone to America but she said she was on her way to see you.'

'That's right, mum. She suddenly turned up this afternoon, right out of the blue.'

'Oh dear. Is everything all right, love. She was in such a funny mood. I couldn't get a sensible word out of her. All she wanted was your address. Was I alright to give it to her?'

'Well mum…in many ways it was a blessing in disguise. It was the excuse I needed to…do something I should have done months ago.'

'And what was that, love?'

'Say goodbye to her. She's gone from my life.'

Mum adopted a worried look and, unusually for her, was momentarily lost for words.

'And…are you all right about that Peter?'

'I'm really happy about it, mum. I couldn't be happier.'

I could see out of the corner of my eye that Amy was smiling at me encouragingly.

'But aren't you a bit …lonely?'

'Not a bit. I'm fine mum, really, I'm fine.'

This was followed by a second brief silence.

'Well, that's good then, Peter. That's the main thing. As long as you're happy (Pause) That's good to hear.'

'Yes mum, everything's fine. Really (Pause). So, was there something else, mum. Something else on your mind?'

96

'No, I don't think so. Not really...so...well, there was one thing. I was just talkin' to somebody the other day and they were tellin' me about a lovely young girl who works in your office. I thought you might like to, you know, just say hello to her.'

This was an unexpected change of direction.

'Oh? What's her name?'

Mum stared intently at the screen.

'Oh, what was it again... oh yes, her name's Amy. That's it, Amy.'

By now Amy's grin had magnified to intense, silent giggles. Good old mum, she'd really got me this time.

'So, who did you say told you this?'

'Oh, just somebody...on the phone, you know.'

I smiled broadly, recognising the signature trademark of my sister's work. 'Now, let me see. Amy...Amy? Yes, the name does ring a bell. As a matter of fact, I have a work colleague with me at the moment. Hang on—I'll ask her. Maybe she knows Amy.'

I slowly rotated the phone so that mum could see a giggling Amy seated opposite me. Amy quickly composed herself and waved.

'Hello Mrs Campbell. I'm Amy. It's lovely to meet you!'

Mum looked delighted beyond words.

'Auch, Amy! And you look every bit as pretty as Annie said you were. But please, just call me Eileen.'

'Thanks...Eileen. Thanks.'

I rotated the phone back to point at my face.

'Excellent detection skills, Mrs Campbell!'

Mum was still smiling broadly. 'Well, lucky for me I have a daughter to keep me in the picture. If I had to rely on my son for basic information, I'd be waitin' 'til it turned up on the BBC news! Anyway, Peter, is Amy...is she your girlfriend now?'

'She is, mum. She's just perfect!' I winked at Amy.

'Oh, she looks lovely Peter but...isn't she a bit young for you. She looks about sixteen!'

'Mum, can I just remind you that I'm on speaker phone here...so Amy can hear every word you say!'

'Oh, sorry dear!'

'She's actually thirteen years…'

'…Oh my God Peter!'

'Let me finish, mum. She's actually 13 years younger than me, which makes her 23. Remember when you were 23 you went off on your own to live in Canada for a year!'

Mum nodded. *'Yes, you're right I suppose.'*

'Tell you what, mum.' I continued. 'Why don't Amy and I pop up to Leamington to see you and dad. I'd really like you to meet her and I know she'd love to meet you both.'

I shot a quizzical glance at Amy who smiled and nodded.

'Oh Peter, that would be just…'

'…shall we come around lunchtime on Sunday?

'Come mid-morning and stay for lunch, why don't you. Your dad and I would love that!'

'Oh, well, if you insist, mum! So, that's great and we'll look forward to seeing you both at around 11 o'clock on Sunday morning.'

'Bye dear. Oh, dad sends his love. 'Bye!'

'Bye.'

'Wow!' said Amy, when I'd put the phone down. 'So, I've finally got to talk to the famous mum—the wise woman of Leamington Spa who always manages to say the right thing in a crisis!'

I laughed loudly. 'Really? *That* mum? I think you should maybe reserve judgement 'til Sunday! Now, I don't know about you, but I'm totally cream crackered!'

Amy nodded, 'Yea, it's been a hell of a day!'

'Let's get to bed, then. I've another busy day tomorrow!'

20

The following day involved another school visit for me in Cambridge so it meant an early start. As Amy was still on sick leave, I didn't want to disturb her. She was asleep as I was about to set off.

I kissed her on the top of her head and whispered, 'À bientôt, ma cherie.'

'À bientôt, mon cher,' she whispered back.

The roads were pleasingly free of traffic at that early hour. I pulled in to fill up with petrol and while at the service station was able to buy eight—yes eight— different daily newspapers. Then I was on my way in the direction of the A421. In the event, I was glad to have set off in good time. The traffic entering Cambridge was nightmarish and I only just made it to the school in time for my lesson.

I was greeted by Maggie Crooks, a former student of mine who had got her first teaching job in a modern and very progressive secondary school just outside Cambridge. She had been an outstanding student and I always knew that she would be a great teacher—dynamic, popular with the kids and ever open to trying out fresh ideas. I'd already visited this particular Y7 class earlier in the term to try out an experimental lesson and found them to be lively and enthusiastic. As it was so near the end of term, with the approval of the head, Maggie was able to wangle a longer than usual session with this class.

As we walked into the classroom, the kids were buzzing with excited banter.

'Have you brought your washing line with you this time, Mr Campbell?'

'What are we doing today, sir? Ironing your shirts?'

and so on.

I began the lesson by addressing the class.

'Did you know that between the Earth and Mars there is a small china teapot revolving around the sun in an elliptical orbit?' I paused.

'How did it get there, sir?'

'No one knows!'

'Is it called planet Teapot?'

'Can it be seen by telescope?'

'No, it's too small!'

'I believe you sir. You're a teacher; you wouldn't lie!'

'No,' I smiled, 'I've never lied in my life!'

'So how can you prove it's there?'

'How can you prove it's not?' I replied.

Then Maggie jumped in …

'Here's another strange thing. There's a family of tiny fairies living in the middle drawer of my bedside table!'

'Have you seen them, miss?'

'No, never!'

'Do you hear them chatting at night?'

'No, they're silent!'

'Does one of them play the trombone, miss?'

Maggie shook her head.

'So how do you know they're there then, miss?'

'Well,' Maggie smiled mysteriously. 'I just have this feeling. You've gotta believe in *something*!'

'Are you remembering to take your medication, miss?'

Then I asked, 'Does anyone else have strange or startling stories?'

Lilac raised her hand. 'I can do readings, sir. I get it from my gran! I can look at people and predict their future!'

'Can you predict mine?' I asked.

'Well, I normally charge a tenner, but …'

'… in the interests of science, Lilac,' Maggie interrupted, 'can you waive your fee this time?'

'Well, gran says it don't work if people don't pay!'

'Please!'

'OK then!' She turned back to face me. 'Well, sir, I can see ... that you are very happy and you're going to have a ... joyful life!'

'Well, that's nice to hear, Lilac. Anything else?'

'Yea, you're gonna earn loads of money.'

'Oh, good-o! And ... any bad things?'

'Well,' Lilac hesitated. 'You're gonna die ...'

Everyone gasped, including me.

'... eventually!' Lilac continued. 'You're gonna die, eventually!'

'But everyone dies eventually!' someone shouted.

'So, Lilac,' I said, 'to summarise, I'm going to live a long, rich and happy life and die an old man.'

Lilac gave me the double thumbs up. 'Tell them what they want to hear! That's what my gran always says!'

These stories set off a very lively discussion and Maggie wrote on the board some of the comments that came up from the children.

predicting,   compared to what?
some things are hard to measure,   who says?
proving,   proving a negative
only hearing what we want to hear

This was all a preamble to the main part of the lesson, where I handed out the newspapers that I had brought. I invited the pupils to take a close look at star signs. Are star sign predictions accurate? Are they consistent across different newspapers? How could you prove it?

Working in groups of 3 or 4, they analysed the astrological predictions printed in each newspaper and then pooled their findings across the entire class. It was certainly a lively lesson that fully engaged the class members.

Over lunch I had the chance to find out what Maggie thought of it all.

'Well, I was slightly surprised that from the start, most of the kids didn't really believe in star signs anyway (It's just a bit of fun, ain't it miss!). But they were certainly surprised at how different some of the predictions were from one newspaper to another (It's all a bit dodgy that they came up with totally different things!). And I think they could see that these questions are largely a matter of interpretation (A lot of these predictions could mean different things to different people!) However, the main plus is that you got them thinking about some important bigger life issues. It makes a change for working through Exercise 47(b), the even numbers, from the maths textbook!'

After lunch I was able to give Amy a buzz to tell her I was just setting off. 'So, any stories for me while I've been away, then,' I asked her.

There was a brief moment of silence before Amy could reply. 'Stories—yes stories!' she replied, slowly.

'Ooh, such as …?' I asked.

'Well … let's wait 'til you get back. I'll tell you everything then.'

21

I got home around 3.30. As I walked through the front door there was a lovely aroma filling the air—the smell of freshly baked bread. I could make out another equally delicious smell but one that I couldn't quite place.

'Home is the hunter!' Amy said, smiling as I walked towards her. Then with an uncharacteristically serious face, she asked, 'Hey Pete, have you ... you know ... missed me?'

I gave her a huge hug. 'Amy, of course I have! You see, the thing is, I love you! Now, what's that unfamiliar but yummy smell doing in our flat?'

'You'll see!' she replied.

I switched on the kettle and then Amy produced a box of brownies that she'd baked during the morning.

'Wow!' I exclaimed. 'La Dolce Vita! Will you be able to stay on for a few more days and cook for me, do you think?' Amy wrinkled her face. 'See how indispensable I'm already becoming to you. This is all part of my grand plan to take over your life!'

We sat down with our coffee and brownies and then I asked, 'So, AC, tell me all about it.' Amy looked away and I could see that she was not her usual bubbly self.

'Not just yet,' she replied. 'It's all too ... I want to hear about your day first.'

So ... I treated her to tales from the classroom and I could see that the various wisecracks and gags from the kids were cheering her up. One particularly tickled her. I had been asking how they would know whether a particular medicine actually worked. I said that last week I'd had a painful back, I took a pill and now it seems better. But was it the pill that cured me or something else? Darren's response to this hypothetical scenario was to remark, "So, sir, are you saying that you had a weak back…about a week back?" She managed a smile at this wisecrack.

Amy removed a small folder from her backpack and placed it on her lap. 'Well,' she said, taking a deep breath, 'here goes! I'm going to tell you about a very deceitful geezer called Maurice Charles John.'

'Let me take you back to May 2019. I was coming to the end of my first year at university. I received a request to see my personal tutor on a matter of urgency. My tutor explained that there had been a medical emergency at home. My father had been hospitalised— struck down by a serious illness. She suggested that I make my way home as quickly as possible. I packed a few things and took an early train the following morning.'

'When I got in, the flat looked like a bomb site. Empty boxes of take-aways, cans of Carling everywhere and unwashed dishes in the sink. Dad was in bed looking very much the worse for wear— unwashed, unshaven and giving off a strong smell of whiskey. He said that he'd been in hospital for several weeks and had just been discharged. He told me that he'd had a brain scan and they weren't sure exactly what was wrong with him but he was led to believe that he may have only a few months left.'

'I felt that I had no choice so I discharged myself from my course and came home to look after him. Quite quickly he started to rally and, as you know, here he is over four years later in the very best of health.'

I looked at Amy askance. 'Have we witnessed a little miracle here … or maybe not … ?'

Amy shook her head. 'Let me show you one of the documents from dad's papers.'

She opened her folder and passed over a hospital report on Maurice Charles John, dated 13th May, 2019.

13 May 2019

Dear Mr John,

In relation to your recent brain scan, you will be pleased to hear that your test results have not shown up any serious underlying condition. We believe that your temporary memory loss was probably linked to mild alcohol poisoning. Provided you can refrain from consuming any alcohol for the next few weeks, we feel confident that you will make a full recovery and be able to get back into your regular routine quite soon. Please use this as an opportunity to make a fresh start: to eat well, exercise to stay in shape, drink alcohol in moderation, and quit smoking if you smoke.

'He would have received this a couple of days before I was called home.'

I sat back in the chair feeling stunned.

'The old bugger! But he didn't mind trampling on *your* dreams in the process.'

Amy nodded sadly.

'So, you never went back to university then?'

'No. That was the end of my university career. Dad sat me down and explained that his health problems were such that he'd…he'd never work again!' She put her head in her hands, trying to recollect exactly the sequence of events.

'So…?'

'So, he told me I had to get a job. And a week later he handed over a letter addressed to me. It was an acceptance for a secretarial post at a local paper mill.'

'What! An *acceptance*…for a job you knew nothing about?'

'That's right.'

'But did you have any…I mean, what about qualifications?'

Amy's eyes filled with tears. 'He said it would be easy—just filing and a bit of typing. And then he handed me a second bulky envelope. It contained an official looking document. "You won't need it but just in case anybody asks, you can show them this." he said. It held a fancy certificate awarded to Amy Carpenter. It seems that I graduated from the secretarial course with A grades in every module. Clever me!'

'And who issued the qualification?'

'It was from a Secretarial College of Des Moines in Iowa—an on-line course, apparently.'

I just couldn't believe what I was hearing. 'But how the hell would your dad get that together. I would have thought a stunt like that would have been way above his pay grade.'

'I don't think he did. He knows a guy called Jimbo. It seems that Jimbo's a whizz at computer design…'

'…otherwise known as document forging.' I interrupted.

'Probably,' Amy nodded.

'So…so you accepted the job offer then?'

'Yes. It was OK. Luckily my A-levels included Computing so my IT skills were pretty good. Apart from that I just bluffed my way and learnt on the job.'

There was a silence as I took in this latest revelation. 'Can I ask, Aims, does anyone else know about what you've just told me?'

Amy shook her head rapidly. 'No, no Pete. Nobody. Please promise you'll not breathe a word of this!'

'I promise. Don't worry. Your secret is safe with me.'

'You see…this became something that I…that dad would sometimes sort of threaten me with. He knew how much I loved working in the faculty but he'd say things like, 'If only they knew the truth about you, my girl. I could get you sacked in a second!'

I shook my head. 'And yet it was all his idea in the first place! How dare he!' She shook her head sadly.

'Amy, you know you said you stuck with your dad because you felt sorry for him and felt he needed looking after.'

She nodded.

'Well, it strikes me that he also sort of had a hold over you about these forged qualifications.'

She nodded again. 'Yes, you're right. It wasn't exactly blackmail but it wasn't a million miles away from it.'

I took her hand. 'I just can't believe that he lied about being too ill to work and then he sent you out to work instead...what a con artist! Never, ever have anything to do with that man again!'

After a pause for quiet reflection for both of us, Amy then said, 'OK. That's one crime. But that's not all.'

She passed me a second document from her folder.

English Bulldog	£2,995
Cavapoo	£2,949
Miniature Dachshund	£2,537
Cockapoo	£2,471
Cavalier King Charles Spaniel	£2,458
French bulldog	£2,389
Pomeranian	£2,247
Dachshund	£2,242
Cocker Spaniel	£2,230
Labrador Retriever	£1,948

'He got this off the Hello Magazine website, dated this year. It was from an article about the most expensive dog breeds in the UK and these are the prices of puppies.'

'Curious!' I said, looking down the list. 'Dog lover, is he, your dad? Perhaps looking to buy a little Cockapoo puppy?'

'Are you kidding? He hates dogs. He hates all pets. To him they're just more work and that's not his style!'

'So, what are you thinking?'

Amy paused before responding. 'I'd say he hasn't acquired this list because he wants to *buy* a puppy. He uses it to decide how much to charge for *selling* them.'

'But where would he get the puppies from?' I asked innocently.

'I don't know for sure but I reckon he steals them! You know all this driving around delivering parcels. My guess is that's a cover for sourcing and then stealing pedigree breeds of puppies.'

'Really!' I gasped. 'But that raises further questions. Where does he keep them—not at home obviously— who does he sell them on to ...?'

Amy interrupted, 'You know we have a garage attached to our flat. I've never been allowed inside it.'

'But he couldn't keep puppies there. You'd have heard them.'

'No, but the garage could be where he stores all his … his …you know … puppy stealing gear.'

'Well, he's clearly not doing this on his own, then. I wonder …'

'Jimbo!' interrupted Amy. 'I bet he's the other half of the racket. If Jimbo lives in a rural spot, he'll have a barn where these poor puppies can bark all night without arousing suspicion. And he'll be the one with a network of potential customers.'

'Hmm, Jimbo again. And if you're right, these stolen puppies would need convincing paperwork to show that they were the genuine article. Sounds like another job for Jimbo the master forger!'

Amy nodded. 'Well, this is all total guesswork, actually, but …'

'Yes,' I cut in, '…but given what we now know about Maurice the Malefactor, it's certainly possible!'

I looked over at her folder and saw that there was a third document awaiting my attention. 'So, what have we here?' I asked. 'His biggest crime of all?'

Amy face revealed no expression.

'I just … I just … don't know where to start with … '

She was unable to complete the sentence.

She passed over the document to me and turned her face away to the wall. It was an undated hand-written letter addressed to Amy's dad. I read it aloud.

Cher Maurice,

I don't know if you will ever read this. I am beyond my mind with worry. Where are you and what have you done with my dearest Chérie? We agreed that we would meet at the station at Lisieux. I waited all day, but nothing. I am so very unhappy, I just can't tell you. Please let me know where you are and that my little chicken is well and safe.

Je suis si tous mentée

I am begging ECX

I placed the letter back on the coffee table and took Amy in my arms. She began to sob—silent sobs at first but slowly these turned into great torrents of uncontrollable weeping.

22

'What a lovely house you have!' said Amy as she stood in the hall and looked around at the wood-panelled walls. 'Wow!'

Mum and dad looked pleased. 'Oh, we bought this place back in the day when houses were much cheaper than they are now,' mum replied. 'We were very lucky really. Would you like the grand tour, Amy?'

Amy grinned and nodded. 'Yes please! I've only ever lived in a little flat. I'm not used to all this space!'

They went up the stairs to inspect the bedrooms and bathroom. I could hear mum's voice going "like ding stour", as she would say. She sounded like an estate agent giving her customer the hard sell.

'So, dad, how have you been yourself?'

'Oh, not bad son. But…these auld knees are still givin' me a hard time. It's got now that I can only drive short distances. Alright to go to the shops but that's about it.'

'Sorry to hear that, dad. And is mum any better?'

'Oh, much the same. She gets very tired—you know, breathless and just no energy. She's on these pills and they do seem to help but it's just…it's just life in the slow lane for both of us these days. But, Peter, tell me, is that Clare out of your life now?'

'Gone, vanished, disappeared without trace…'

'…and replaced, I see!' dad interrupted.

I laughed. 'I hope you'll like Amy, dad. She's very different to Clare. You'll find her shy but very kind-hearted.'

Dad smiled, 'Yes indeed, that would make her *very* different to the other one, then! You know, she quite upset your mother on the phone the other day. Very brusque and completely lacking in…'

'Good manners?' I interjected.

Dad nodded. 'So anyway, shy is good. Sure, I'm shy myself and there's nothin' wrong with that. When you're with people you care about, shyness doesn't last. Back home we used to say that shyness goes when you realise no one's lookin'! It just means we'll take our time gettin' to know her, and that's a good thing.'

It wasn't long before we could hear the return of the ladies. Amy grinned at me, 'What a view out the back Pete! Oh, your mum pulled down that wooden ladder thingy and I got a peep at your old attic bedroom.'

I smiled. 'Yea, that was where I used to get locked away by these two. Luckily, I had my TV, my computer, and my guitar up there. I was only allowed out for the occasional meal…and of course to do all those chores I've been telling you about.'

'Hah,' said dad, laughing. 'You're quare craic young fella-me-lad! *You,* doin' the chores? I musta been away that day!'

We walked through to the kitchen/dining area at the back of the house. Amy went straight over to the large French windows. 'It's a lovely garden, Mr Campbell! I saw it from upstairs.'

'Oh please, Amy, it's Jimmy. Call me Jimmy. Yes, the garden was what really sold us the house. It was perfect for the wains to play in. And on top of that, there's the meadow area beyond the fence so they used to have the run of that as well.'

Mum walked over to join Amy. 'No wains to play in it now, sadly, except when the boys come down, of course. But it's still Jimmy's pride and joy. He just loves it.'

Dad took Amy's arm. 'Come on 'til you see it, Amy. Are you a gardener yourself?'

'No, but I love cooking.'

'Oh, then you'll be wantin' to see my vegetable plot! I've got everything into raised beds these days. It makes it so much easier to keep it all under control!'

I put my arm on mum's shoulder and we watched as dad took Amy on an extensive tour of his lovely garden. We could see that he was really on a roll—chat, chat, chat! All Amy had to do was just smile and nod.

Mum filled the kettle and switched it on. 'She's settlin' in great, isn't she!' she said with a smile. 'I thought she was going' to be…you know… a bit shy.'

'What made you think that?'

'Oh, um… Annie may have mentioned it! But…you know, Peter, I think we're gonna like your Amy. She's got a kind face.'

I gave her arm a squeeze. 'I know you will, mum. She's got a kind heart too. But, one thing I wanted to say, though. She hasn't had that easy a childhood. Can you do me a favour and try not to ask her too much about her family.'

Mum gave me a sympathetic smile. 'Auch I'm really sorry to hear that. But you can count on me, so you can. My reputation for tact and discretion is legendary!'

I gave her a wry look. 'Yes mum…that was what I was afraid of!'

Fifteen minutes later, the four of us were sitting down to a cup of tea with a large plate of home-made oatmeal biscuits placed in front of us. 'Eat up, eat up, Amy!' said mum. 'Sure, lunch won't be for another hour at least!'

We all laughed at that one.

'Oh, by the way, Amy,' she continued. 'I hope you like chicken. That's what's on the menu for lunch.'

Amy smiled. 'Thanks Eileen. That'll be great. "Winner, winner chicken dinner"—that's what Sam says, isn't it?'

'Ha ha,' laughed mum, delighted to be already sharing with her visitor a conversation about the wonder that is Sam. 'He does indeed. He does indeed! Auch, he's a great wee fellow. And so's Harry. Lovely boys. Of course you've met them.'

'I have. They taught me how to ride a bike!' Amy replied. Dad laughed. 'Oh, we know, we know. They told us all about it! There isn't too much gets past this family!'

I looked over at Amy and was pleased to see a look of quiet contentment on her face. As mid-morning tea gradually morphed into lunch, she sat quietly watching and listening. She seemed to be at ease sitting in on the copious anecdotes and gossip, both ancient and modern, about the life and times of the Campbell family.

Then mum turned to Amy. 'We're very rude, love. Here we are goin' on and on about people you've never heard of!' Amy smiled. 'Not a bit, Eileen. I'm just loving this! You see...well, I don't really have a family of my own. So...all this is new to me.'

'So, you don't have any siblings, then, Amy?' dad asked.

Amy shook her head. 'No. And my mum died about twenty years ago. So, there's just me and my dad.'

'I'm so sorry to hear that, Amy,' said mum. This was quickly followed by 'Auch, that's such a sadness for you, love,' from dad. There was a silence for a few moments and I could see mum wrestling with her natural urge to wade in and give some of her legendary tact and discretion a serious workout. I decided that a change of tack was required.

'Anyway, dad, I was just wondering...are you still playing the piano these days? Maybe you'll give us a bit of recital after lunch?' Dad shook his head. 'Oh no. I don't play so much now, Peter. What with the garden and everything else I don't seem to have the time.'

'Hah!' I laughed. 'The perpetual cry of the retiree. Just too busy not going out to work to do the fun stuff!'

Dad laughed.

'I'd really love to hear you play, Jimmy' said Amy shyly. 'Please!'

I could see that dad was quite delighted to be asked so after all traces of lunch had been expunged and we had retreated to the sitting room, he went next door and came back with an armful of battered songbooks. He set them on Amy's lap. 'You mightn't know any of these songs, Amy. They're probably all long before your time.'

Amy leafed excitedly through them—'Beatles, Queen, James Taylor...these are great, Jimmy! I know loads of these songs!' She giggled, 'I'm a bit of an old-fashioned girl, actually!'

Dad was in his element. He opened the page at Bohemian Rhapsody by Queen and set it up on the music rest above the open piano lid. We all gathered round. 'Let's see what youse can all do with this one, then,' he grinned.

And so it continued for the next hour. None of us could believe how many of these "ancient" songs Amy knew and, with us all singing together, she really belted it out. As we were just ready to call it a day, dad turned to Amy and said, 'You've got a voice on you there, love!'

Amy smiled modestly. Then dad continued. 'Tell you what, Amy; there's a Beatles song that really means something special to me. It's called *In my life.*' He sang a couple of bars of it. She smiled and said, 'Oh yes—beautiful song. I do know it.'

'Great, right then, everyone else shut up. Amy and I are goin' to do this one on our own.'

Amy's eyes widened. 'Are we?' she asked, but dad had already started playing the introduction. Having no say in the matter she came in with the opening verse.

There are places I'll remember
All my life, though some have changed.
Some forever, not for better;
Some have gone and some remain.

All these places had their moments
With lovers and friends I still can recall.
Some are dead and some are living,
In my life I've loved them all.

Then they started the second verse and this time dad joined in, softly singing the harmony. As he did so, Amy reached out and grabbed my hand.

But of all these friends and lovers
There is no one compares with you.
And these mem'ries lose their meaning
When I think of love as something new.

Tho' I know I'll never lose affection
For people and things that went before,
I know I'll often stop and think about them,
In my life I love you more.

When they'd finished, dad turned in his chair to face his singing partner and I could see real emotion in his face. 'That was… lovely, Amy. Thank you!'

23

We pushed open the wrought iron gate and walked up the path along the side of Marta's house to enter her lovely garden. Prior to her retirement, it had always looked rather chaotic but over the past year she had really thrown herself into gardening. The flowers were starting to outnumber the weeds, five raised beds containing vegetables and fruit had been added and the recently mown lawn had never looked greener.

Seated next to Marta at a wooden garden table was Annette Dupont, lecturer in French at the university and longtime buddy of Marta. After hugs and kisses were exchanged, Amy and I sat down with them at the table.

Amy turned to Annette. 'Lovely to meet you, Annette. Thanks so much for agreeing to chat to us!'

Annette smiled back at us. 'Oh, I'm delighted to be here and meet you both. I just hope I can help you in some little way, Amy!'

As we helped ourselves to the fruit juice and biscuits laid out on the table, Amy suddenly said 'Well, here we are, the four of us, in this lovely English country garden … and it turns out that … not one of us is actually English!' After a moment's silence, everyone burst out laughing. Well, it certainly broke the ice!

'Amy,' said Annette, still smiling, 'Marta has told me a bit about your situation. I'm so sorry. But how marvellous that you managed to get your hands on your French *acte de naissance*!'

'I can't tell you how exciting that was, Annette,' Amy replied with a huge smile. She removed the birth certificate from her folder and handed it over to Annette.

Annette studied it carefully.

'Aimée Clotilde! What lovely names you have my dear. I'm sure great thought went into their choosing.'

I could see Amy's eyes welling up at this remark and she was just able to mouth the words, 'Thank you so much!' Then she pointed to the final entry on the document, *lieu de la reconnaissance.*

'I wasn't sure about the word *reconnaissance*,' she said. 'I thought it meant "place of recognition" but that doesn't make sense.'

'It does mean that,' replied Annette, 'but on this document it refers to place of registration. So, your birth was registered in Lisieux—a very beautiful little city …'

'… suggesting that perhaps Amy was born near there?' I asked.

'Yes, maybe,' replied Annette, 'though sometimes people are prepared to travel some considerable distance if they wish their baby's registration to be in a place that is of special significance to them.'

'So, Amy,' Marta said slowly, 'I have question and I feel I must have to ask. You think your mother maybe still … alive?'

There was a long pause as Amy gathered her thoughts. Eventually she said 'I have only one source of information saying that she has died, and that is my father. But honestly, his credibility is zero. I now know that nothing he's ever told me about my family is true. And I think that he may have told me she was dead to stop me looking for her. Of course I want her to be alive. I want that so much. But wanting it doesn't make it true.'

'No,' said Annette, 'but at least you have enough reason to start looking!'

'You bet!' said Amy enthusiastically. 'I just can't wait to get started!'

'As far as you know, Amy,' Marta asked, 'you were only child?'

Amy nodded.

'But is possible your mum have further children after you.'

Amy's eyes widened in shock at this thought. 'Oh my God. I never even thought about that! I might have a sister, or a brother … or both!'

117

Marta continued. 'Amy, I suggested you meet up with Annette as she specially interest in 20th century French history. And I must tell you she shit-hot to searching out historical links between people.'

Annette smiled at Marta 'Shit hot! Thanks Marta! I need to put that testimonial onto my CV!' Then she looked intently at Amy.

'Look, my dear, if you really do have a mystery family living in France, I'll do what I can to help you find them. When I was younger, I spent a lot of time chasing down people's records from a great variety of local sources. I used to travel all over to visit dusty archives! But that's changed now. The truth is that these days your two best weapons are the computer and DNA testing. You'll want to sign up to an online genealogy platform. Choose one that has a really large database of records. But I need to give you some bad news here. Accessing contemporary French DNA data is very problematic. One small point, though. If you can't find your mother quickly, don't be too discouraged because that's perhaps a good thing!'

Amy looked confused. 'But why?'

'Well, these sites are usually happier to allow public access to the genealogical records of people who have already died. But for people who are still living, they are much more circumspect. As it happens, French law is quite strict on this matter, which makes it particularly hard to track down someone in France who is still alive.'

Amy looked disappointed at this news. Then she said, 'But, Annette, if my mum were alive and really wanted to find me, isn't it possible that she will include her details on some site where it will make it easier for me to find her?'

Annette smiled. 'Well, if she is tech-savvy, that is what I would hope for! But also, there might be a relative that you have in common. It's how it often works in practice! In your mother's case I'm sure she will really want to be found!'

Amy looked relieved. 'Thank you so much!'

At this point, Annette invited Amy to join her for a 'tour of the estate'. They set off slowly in the direction of the vegetable area and immediately began talking in very rapid and animated French.

Within seconds, I could see that Amy had started to pick up Annette's busy Gallic 'armography'. She looked like a different person—happier than I had ever seen her and without the slightest hint of her debilitating shyness.

Marta got up from her seat and moved around the table to sit down beside me. 'Just look those two,' she said, smiling with pleasure. 'Whatever happened to nervous young woman who visit my house just short while ago!'

'Yes,' I laughed, 'When I first met Amy, her life was relatively calm and uneventful. Now, suddenly, it's turned into a crazy soap opera!'

'But I'm so thrilled for her,' said Marta enthusiastically. 'Yes, is roller-coaster ride but she is young and energetic. And…is wonderful how you're both to do it together!'

'Well, one of the discoveries I've made about Amy is that beneath that veil of shyness is a highly intelligent and extremely…funny person. I feel so lucky! As well as being the partner I love, she is also a highly entertaining companion.'

Marta beamed at me. 'Yes, I can see. And I'm so happy for both of you!' Then she changed gear and looked at me seriously. 'You know, Peter, when you last came to house with Amy, I thought maybe…maybe things not very happy at home for her. How is progressing there?'

I reassured Marta that Amy had indeed moved on considerably. I told her about our 'breaking and entering' of Amy's father's valuables drawer. She couldn't believe the lucky find of a passport in Amy's name but she did point out that there may be problems ahead with the mismatch between the names on her passport and on her birth certificate.

'And what about Amy's father?' Marta then asked. 'She has been contacting to him since she left?'

'This is a tricky one,' I replied. 'In theory he should be a goldmine of important information about Amy's mother and of her past life in France. But would he tell her anything? Amy thinks not and I agree with her. She really wants nothing more to do with him.'

Marta nodded thoughtfully. 'Do you think he might come look for her? What if he just turning up to her office?'

'Well, that is a worry for her. Yes, she thinks he might come looking for her but…one good thing is that these days campus security is pretty tight so visitors can't just walk in willy-nilly like they used to. She's also placed his name on a university 'watch list' so security know about him!'

'What if he might got as far as faculty building?'

'Well, we've briefed all of Amy's immediate colleagues and also she's got herself a new internal phone number.'

At that moment the French branch of the garden inspectorate came back from their perambulations and joined us. Both were in high spirits.

'Ah-ha!' said Marta, 'The return of sisters of revolution! Vive la France!'

Amy grinned and nodded at Annette. 'That chat was so helpful! I know I'll need to sit at the computer but Annette has given me lots of other suggestions. If my mother thought that I might still be in France, she may have used a variety of search options local to Normandy.'

'So, you'll really need to be there in situ, I suppose,' I said grinning at her. 'I just hope you're not going to drag me over to Normandy! You know how much I hate it there! But, having said that, Amy,' I continued in a more serious tone, 'next week Annie and Ben and the boys will be in Slieve Gallion. Given that you now have a passport, can you give me one good reason why we shouldn't join them?'

Amy's jaw dropped. 'Well, perhaps Stacey?'

'As a matter of fact, I've already had a word with Stacey to confirm booking next week off for myself and her exact words were "Shall I make that two?"'

24

It had been a very early start to catch the 8.15am ferry from Portsmouth but that had done nothing to dampen Amy's excitement levels, which had been off the scale ever since we set out from Milton Keynes. I was excited too but witnessing it though her eyes made me feel like I was reliving all my childhood visits to France rolled into one. For Amy there was an extra set of emotional layers—she was setting out for her childhood home, she was returning to the country of her birth and of course most poignant of all, she was approaching the place where she last saw her mother. I knew it would only be a matter of time before the full import of these interconnected emotional elements would collide. It happened about five hours into the crossing. I was in the queue for a final coffee when she tapped my arm and said 'just popping up on deck. I see land!'

'Righty ho. See you in a bit. '

I returned to our table with the coffees and could make her out through the window—a solitary, wind-blown figure leaning on the rail taking in the expanding image of the French coastline as it rolled towards her. I decided to let her make this part of her emotional pilgrimage in private. Ten minutes later, when her coffee had gone cold, I walked outside to join her. I put my arms around her and kissed the back of her neck. I looked around the side of her head and could see tears streaming down her face. I hugged her tightly. She squeezed my hand in response.

'We've just had the call.' I whispered. 'Time to go to the car deck!'

She turned, wiped her cheeks and kissed me.

'Let's go! 'she replied, smiling through her tears.

We drove from the port at Ouistreham, heading south-east towards Slieve Gallion. Having made this odyssey every summer, for practically all of my thirty-six years, I knew the route intimately. Family tradition dictated that the manner of our travel to our second home was every bit as important as staying there. So, like my parents before me, I avoided main roads. As we drove off the ferry, I immediately turned left around the dilapidated fair and then across the "rickety rickety bridge" to join a tiny road that ran parallel to the main road. This was the start of Amy's first proper look at rural France–winding lanes, hedgerows, fields containing cows and countless ancient, beamed barns that were in imminent state of collapse. We passed through tiny, deserted villages that were totally devoid of people but, if you were lucky, where you might get a friendly wag of a tail from a passing dog.

'Welcome to 1958, Mme Charpentier! 'I said and Amy just smiled. We spent the rest of the journey in almost total silence with Amy staring out of the window taking it all in. At one point, she glanced across at me and smiled. I patted her knee gently.

Just over an hour later we entered the tiny hamlet of Crissay. The gates had already been left open for us and I swung into the yard, rattled across the stones and parked alongside Annie and Ben's car. 'Welcome to Slieve Gallion, Aims!' She threw her arms around my neck and kissed both my cheeks.

I was seated under the giant tree that dominates the back yard in Slieve Gallion, pretending to be working on my iPad but in reality just chilling and playing *All of You*. Harry walked past and glanced at my screen.

'Still doing your very 'portant work, I see, Uncle Pete!'

'Ah yes Harry, this bloomin' thesis just seems to dominate my thoughts night and day!'

Harry took a closer look at my screen. 'How many chickens have you got now?'

'Oh, I'm up to 23 actually,' I said rather guiltily.

'That's very good, Uncle Pete. I've just been playing it with Amy on her laptop…'

'Oh, yes? Going well?'

'Yup. We're on 67. Very nearly finished it!'

'Oh, thanks Harry. Good to know! That's very confidence building!'

I decided to abandon all pretence and wandered over to join Amy, Annie and Ben who were all seated at the table, hiding from the sun and sipping iced lemonade. I poured myself a glass. Amy smiled at Annie. 'How the other half lives, eh?'

'Yes, but it's so damn hot. It's always boiling at this time of the year in Normandy. I have to slather the boys in sun cream and make sure they wear their sun hats.

A few minutes later, Sam came to join us.

'Amy, Amy, you haven't painted yours yet?'

'Sorry Sam, do you mean have I painted my nails?' she asked.

'No, no!' Sam gave her a look of total disbelief that she could be so slow on the uptake. 'Your boat, your boat! We're having the big boat race this afternoon. You're going to have to get a move on! What about you Uncle Pete? Have you done yours?'

I looked at my fingernails, teasingly, and said 'Er, not yet Sam. But it's definitely on my list of things to do!'

'Is there a prize?' Amy asked.

'Of course,' replied Harry. 'The annual trophy!'

He dashed into the house and seconds later came out clutching a tiny, peeling, gold-coloured plastic trophy that had clearly seen better days. Mummy's the current holder—she won it last year!'

'Ooh! You never told us, Annie!' I joked. 'I had no idea! Modest to a fault, as usual!'

Annie raised her eyes briefly from her iPad and replied 'I've got a lot of hidden talents that you know nothing about, boyo!'

Relaxing in the back yard of Slieve Gallion after lunch with a glass of wine, it was hard to conjure up a sense of urgency about anything. But it was clear that Harry and Sam weren't going to allow any more backsliding or procrastination. They had managed to galvanise Annie and Ben who agreed to abandon their iPads to tackle the annual community event.

'OK then boys,' said Ben. 'Let's find our boats and paints and we'll get to work straightaway!'

An hour later we had all finished our masterpieces. Amy had created something quite unusual—it was covered with fish of every size, type and hue and she called it *Fishy-o-Fish*. My own efforts were much more modest. I decided to create a collection of mathematical shapes that fitted together geometrically and I called it *Pete's Tesselation*. Sam produced a creation in pink linked to his favourite toy which he called *The Kirby Award* while Harry went for an impressively flowing composition that bore the name *Rapid River*. Ben drew a series of brightly coloured lightning bolts that looked like something from Battle of the Planets which he called *The Flash*. Annie opted for a vision in green; with no thought of streamlining her craft or considerations of animal health and safety, she somehow managed to attach two small furry creatures to the prow of her boat which she named *The Owl and the Pussycat*.

Sam and Annie were positioned upstream at the starting point. They both stood in the fast-flowing torrent which came almost up to Sam's ankles. Harry was on the bank beside them holding Annie's phone. As he had done a few weeks before when Amy was perfecting her commando roll at the boys' cycling school, he had it set to 'stopwatch' mode. Beside him on the grass lay his pencil and notebook where he had already drawn out a two-way table with the six boat names listed in order of owners' age—from youngest to oldest.

Ben was positioned downstream and had been assigned the crucial role of boat catcher. Meanwhile Amy and I had both adopted the even more important roles of watching, applauding, cheering and generally creating as much enthusiastic hysteria as we could muster.

'Let the race begin!' Ben announced portentously.

Annie released each boat in turn. Sam, holding a long stick, splashed along behind. When a boat got caught in the weeds, which it seemed to do surprisingly often, he would give it a poke with his stick. 'Go on, give it a good poke Sam!' Annie kept advising him at regular intervals. This directive seemed to be particularly in evidence when he was unsticking *The Kirby Award*! Meanwhile, Harry called out the time every five seconds while the rest of us cheered and clapped each boat in turn towards its destination. When the boat catcher shouted 'Home!', Harry stopped his timer, announced the time and then wrote it down into his notebook.

After all six boats had completed their journeys, everyone agreed that it was over far too quickly and we voted for a re-run. In the end, each boat got three chances to strut its stuff on the mighty Orbiquet river.

The annual regatta had always been part of my own childhood holidays in Slieve Gallion. I could still remember vividly my own excitement at winning the coveted trophy when I was about six years of age. But for Amy this was totally new territory. As I watched her scream and cheer and yo-ho, it struck me that she had almost certainly never enjoyed this sort of experience in her entire life. Concepts like fun, like family and like fun-with-family were precious gifts to be cherished. I vowed to share many more of these moments with her in the future.

After the final rerun, Annie, Ben, Harry and Sam went into a huddle to work out the overall results. In the brief interlude, I leaned over and kissed the back of Amy's neck. 'Je t'aime, Aimée Clotilde Charpentier,' I whispered. She turned her head and stared deep into my eyes. Then she kissed me gently on the lips. 'Et je t'aime pour toujours, mon cher!'

'Settle down everyone, settle down!' Harry called out to the assembled multitude. 'It's time for the results!'

We all gathered around the white circular table that stood in the yard. 'Now remember, these results are not about the artwork. If it was about prettiness, *Rapid River* would be the clear winner!'

'No, it wouldn't!' shouted Sam. 'Amy's was the prettiest one … by far!'

'Hear, hear,' shouted Amy. 'At last, someone who understands art. Thank you, Sam!'

'Anyway, here are the results,' continued Harry. In sixth place, with *Pete's Tesselations*, was … Uncle Pete!'

Applause and much cheering.

Sam gave me a hug. 'Better luck next year, Uncle Pete!'

'In a surprising fifth place was last year's winner, mummy with *The Owl and the Pussycat*.'

'I told you, dearest wife,' shouted Ben, 'aerodynamically speaking it was a disaster, darling!'

'In fourth was … me with *Rapid River*! You see Sam poked it with his stick and it never worked properly after that…'

'…get on with it, Harry,' I interrupted.

'Well, in third place was … Amy with *Fishy-o-Fish*!'

'Too pretty!' shouted Annie. 'It didn't have the firepower!'

'Second place went to … Daddy with *The Flash*!'

'Well done daddy, you're normally last!' shouted Sam supportively.

'So, we come to this year's surprising winner and that is … Mister … erm… let me poke it along with my stick, why don't I, … Sam with … *The Kirby Award*!'

Amid wild cheering, Sam delightedly held his trophy aloft. Ben then lifted him up onto his shoulders and paraded him around the garden. Many photos were taken of the winner holding his trophy and then cradling his river-stained pink craft in his arms. As I watched him grinning and waving, I thought to myself, Sam, thirty years from now I bet you'll still remember this moment with total clarity.

25

Early the following morning, Annie, Ben and the boys piled into their car. It was Monday and family tradition dictated that attendance was compulsory at the weekly market in Saint-Pierre-sur-Dîves. Amy and I followed on behind but we were on a rather different mission from that of doing the weekly fruit and vegetable shopping.

We were able to park both cars quite close to the market and opened the boots. Annie and Ben had brought shopping baskets and a large carrier bag. Amy and I fished out several items less associated with a shopping trip—a guitar, a folding kitchen stool, a large placard on a pole and a backpack containing 2000 leaflets. Sam was flabbergasted.

'What … what's going on? Are you two giving a concert at the market?'

Amy smiled at him. 'Well, something like that. We rather hoped you guys could really get the party going and draw a large crowd for us.'

The boys exchanged rather nervous looks. 'Well,' said Sam, 'we'll maybe watch …'

'… from a safe distance!' added Harry.

We left the main street and walked into the market square. On the right hand side was the huge medieval hall, glistening in the sunlight.

'Wow!' said Amy. 'What is *that*!?'

I let her take it in for a few moments before replying. 'Yea, I just love it too. That's the famous *Halles de Saint-Pierre-sur-Dîves*—the market hall. Back in the 11th century, the monks from the abbey used it to sell their goods to the locals.'

Amy looked amazed. 'Eleventh century? But it's in such perfect condition!'

'Well, it's had a few makeovers in the last thousand years. It was completely destroyed by fire when the Germans withdrew from occupation in 1944 but the local community rebuilt it using the same materials— even the wooden beams were of chestnut, just as in the original. But it still forms the heartbeat of this market square and it'll be full of stall holders already hard at it selling their goods.'

'Like what?'

'Oh, mostly fruit, vegetables, local cheese, as well as loads of other stuff—maybe the odd live chicken or rabbit!'

Amy smiled at me. 'Can't wait to see inside—but not yet. We've got a job to do!'

We entered the open-air part of the market and found a relatively quiet spot slightly removed from the milling throng. I knew that what we were about to do was massively outside Amy's comfort zone but this was all her idea and she seemed determined to go through with it. Suddenly she tugged on my arm and said 'Pete, tell me honestly, do you think I'm mad? This is a crazy thing to be doing, isn't it?'

I smiled at her. 'Nope, it's not crazy. You might say it's brave but you know you can do this. Just give it a go but if it doesn't come off, so what? At least you'll have tried!'

Amy did her best to respond with a cheerful grin. 'Yea, you're right. Let's just do it!'

Over the previous week, Amy had worked on creating new lyrics to the song *Where is my Mind*, by The Pixies,

In English, the lyrics she had written were:

I was stolen 19 years ago.
I haven't seen my mother since all this time.
I was taken to live in England (and I ask myself)
Where is my mother?
I've lost my mother!
Have you seen my mother?
She could be your neighbour.

What Amy planned to sing was her French translation: <u>Où est ma mère.</u>

On m'a enlevé il y a dix-neuf ans
Je n'ai pas vu ma mère depuis tout ce temps
J'ai été forcé de vivre en Angleterre
(et je me demande)
Où est ma mère?
J'ai perdu ma mère!
Avez-vous vu ma mère?
Peut-être est-elle votre voisine.

She set up her stool and stepped onto it. Over her left shoulder she held her placard. It displayed a large, recent photograph of Amy and the text read:

À l'aide !
Avez-vous vu ma mère?
Elle s'appelle
Élise Camille Charpentier
Peut-être qu'elle me ressemble.

In her right hand were a bunch of A5 leaflets. We'd had 2000 of these printed at Next Day Printing just a couple of days previously. The leaflets bore the same photo and message as the placard but with the additional contact information of my mobile number and email address. I'd created a new email address especially for the occasion:
ou-est-ma-mere@gmail.com

I began slowly to strum my guitar with the chords— E, C#m, G#, A —and she began to sing. Her voice was just a faint whisper.
On m'a enlevé il y a dix-huit ans...
Suddenly she stopped and put her hand to her mouth. I stopped strumming and looked at her, concerned.
'I can't Pete. My voice has gone,' she whispered and stepped down from the stool. I'd had no way of knowing what would be coming out of her mouth when the pressure was on. We'd rehearsed

the song a few times and she had always sung in a reserved and *sotto voce* manner. But this soft whisper was totally new and rather scary.

'No problem, Aims,' I said, trying to look much more positive than I felt. 'Why don't I sing and you join in when you can.'

I started strumming once more and began to sing the verse. Luckily, we'd rehearsed it enough that I could more or less remember the lyrics. To my great relief, halfway through the verse I could see Amy climb back onto the stool. I grinned at her more in relief than in support! As I hit the chorus, I could hear a little voice join in. When we reached the final line, I went straight back to the start. By now, thank the Lord, Amy was finding her voice and was starting to sing with a little more volume. Third time through, I left her to sing it on her own.

I decided just to keep going. With each passing verse her voice was gradually gaining in strength. I also noticed that her performance was starting to acquire a little more panache and intensity. I could see and hear that the timbre of her voice was changing and that Amy was discovering a new phenomenon—the notion of using her singing voice as a tool for communication. By the fifth time around she wasn't just singing the song to herself—she was starting to perform with real passion to the good people of Saint-Pierre-sur-Dîves.

Up to this point, Annie and Ben had been looking on with some concern. Now they began clapping supportively and the boys moved a little closer.

I could see that several of the shoppers were starting to notice and began drifting across to where we were standing. By the end of the sixth performance, there were several shouts of 'Bravo!' Amy was ready for another round. By the end of the chorus there were over twenty onlookers and several started to come up to talk to her. 'C'est vrai?' one asked. Amy stepped down from her stool.

'Oui, c'est vrai,' she nodded. 'Je cherche ma mère.'

She started handing out the leaflets as more people came across to see what was going on. I began to strum the chords for another time and Amy hopped back onto her stool. None of the existing group of onlookers departed as more and more shoppers moved to join us. Some even began to join in the chorus—Où est sa mère?, Où est sa mère?

Soon she was being swamped with questions. As she handed out the leaflets, Amy tried her best to explain what had happened to her nearly twenty years before. More and more questions were fired at her.

'*Do you remember her? What's your name? Where did you live in France? Where did you last see her? Are you French or English?*' On and on it went!

Luckily Amy's French was well up to the inquisition and she answered all their questions with a smile, even though for most of them she just had to say 'Je ne sais pas'—I don't know.

By now there were 50 or 60 people circled around her stool, all extremely curious about this unusual young woman who had chosen to sing her life story. Some of the late arrivals started shouting, 'Encore, encore!' Amy obligingly climbed back up onto her podium and gave the crowd what they wanted to hear—several more verses of her song.

I could see that Amy had conquered her 'first night nerves' and was starting to look and sound comfortable in what she was doing. For the first time I felt able, in my mind, to step away from the event and listen properly to her singing. Clearly, I am biased when it comes to anything that Amy might do but the timbre of her newly-discovered public voice was quite striking. She was now singing with an intensity that was really connecting with her audience. Looking around at their faces, it was clear that they were loving what they were hearing. When she got to the chorus, everyone started singing 'Où est sa mère? Où est sa mère?' The sound was startling, and Amy had to sing even louder to be heard above the din.

Suddenly two large gendarmes broke through the circle and walked sternly up to me and Amy. Accompanied by a lot of arm-waving and Gallic shrugging they explained that without a busker's licence we were unable to perform. They also pointed out that we were creating a disturbance that could be a danger to public order. I guess they did have a point. However, in my experience, the French public don't have a great love of authority and this interruption was

131

met with noisy shouting, whistling and cat-calling from the onlookers. Things were starting to get rather out of hand and I could see that both gendarmes were beginning to look uneasy. Since Amy and I were the people who had set this hare running in the first place, I felt that we were the ones best placed to finish it with dignity. I whispered to Amy who went over to the gendarmes to make our peace offering in French. The younger one didn't look sure about her suggestion but his older colleague quickly saw that this could be a good way out and reluctantly nodded in agreement. Amy climbed back onto her stool and motioned with her hands to quieten the din. She quickly achieved a total and rather eerie silence. In her excellent French, she said:

'My friends, thank you so much for your support. It is very much appreciated. Please take one of my leaflets and show it to all your friends to help me find my missing mother. Now, our helpful gendarmes have said that they are sorry they arrived so late to the… to the party that they missed out on the opportunity to sing Où est ma mère? with us….'

This comment was met with raucous laughter, applause and slightly embarrassed looks from the two policemen.

Amy continued '… and they have asked … if we can all sing it together just one last time before we…before we disperse.'

The crowd began to cheer. The general mood had by now completely changed and amid much laughter we all hit the song for a final time. Fortunately, the gendarmes were by now enjoying the joke and, in fairness, entered into the singing of the chorus as best they could. Afterwards they both came over to shake hands and even took away a handful of our leaflets for their colleagues. Dozens more leaflets were taken by the remaining onlookers and Amy received many handshakes and wishes of "Bon courage!" Gradually the throng dispersed until there were just the six of us remaining at our post by the kitchen stool.

Both boys rushed to Amy and gave her a massive hug. 'You were brilliant Amy. We'd no idea you could sing like that!' Amy hugged them back. 'As a matter of fact, neither did I!' she laughed.

26

Shopping that morning at the Saint-Pierre-sur-Dîves Monday market proved to be every bit as much fun as I'd ever known it. Annie and the gang had decided to take in the antique stalls so Amy and I made a start by checking out the fruit and vegetables.

The sun was shining, the shoppers were out in large numbers, the noise of their chatter and the cries of the stall vendors were intoxicating. The whole scenario was so…well…so incredibly French! Amy loved every moment of it and held my arm tightly. She loved chatting to the stall holders and was amazed at the very high quality of their produce.

She commented 'At home the supermarket fruit and vegetables tend to be of high quality but at farmers' markets I find that they tend to be a bit …well…ropy. But in France it seems to be the reverse!' I had to agree with her there.

As we tramped from stall to stall, we were still lugging the paraphernalia of our musical adventure—me with my guitar and fold-up stool and Amy with her placard over her shoulder. These items made us instantly recognisable to everyone who had watched us perform and we drew many friendly *saluts* and warm, supportive comments from passersby. I noticed that Amy's encouraging smile particularly attracted the attention of older female shoppers. They would stop to embrace her and look deep into her eyes. 'Bon courage, ma cherie!' I really got the impression that the legend of Aimée Clotilde Charpentier was the biggest story in Saint-Pierre-sur Dîves that morning, if not that decade!

Another timeless family tradition associated with the Monday market in Saint-Pierre has been the compulsory meeting up at a nearby bar—le Brasserie des Halles—for a recuperating drink of coffee or, if it was very hot, a glass of cold Kronenbourg 1664. As we sat waiting for Ben, Annie and the boys to join us, we tried to bag some chairs using the guitar and placard as props. This made these items rather more visible than ever and further drew the attention of the passing public to us. Many of them stopped to ask Amy for some of her leaflets and offered further words of support for her quest.

After a few minutes, two young women came up to us and asked if they could chat about our search for Amy's mother. They introduced themselves as Lili and Juliette from Radio Calvados and said that they presented a weekly current affairs programme. This week it was going to be on tractors but someone had just shown them our leaflet and they thought that Amy's story would be far more interesting. They wondered if she would agree to take part. Of course, Amy was aware that any such publicity would be like gold dust and immediately wanted to be involved.

They proposed a two-staged plan. First, they asked if we would be available that afternoon to come to their smaller local studio in Saint-Pierre and record her song. They further suggested that, later in the week, we might agree to take part in a phone-in where listeners could make direct contact with Amy and, well, just see what happened. This would take place in their main studio in Lisieux.

Amy was over the moon about these proposals and we immediately gave Lili and Juliette the double thumbs up! They provided us with a business card which contained addresses of the two studios as well as contact numbers for both of them. We agreed a time of 2PM for the recording of the song. Lili then produced an iPhone and snapped us both sipping a coffee and giving her the thumbs-up. 'À bientôt!' they called to us as they waved goodbye. 'À bientôt!' we replied, waving back.

Then Amy took my hand and said 'Hey, big boy. Close your eyes and pucker up! Do you know what's coming your way? A couple of hot kisses à la mode française.'

I raised my eyebrows. Really? Here? Mme Charpentier, you are a very modern young woman!'

134

'Oui!' she replied. 'Now, lick your lips and part them slightly!'

I did as I was instructed. Then Amy leaned across the table and, ignoring my trembling lips entirely, planted a French bise on each cheek.

'Very saucy,' I said laughing.

'If you want saucy, you'll have to wait 'til this evening!' Amy grinned back.

I texted Annie that we were at the bar and she texted straight back, 'Be there in 5 mins!'

We ordered drinks and pastries for six and just as these were being brought to our table, the gang of four arrived. Excitement levels were still off the scale with the boys and of course Amy remained very much the centre of attention.

After Annie and the gang had set off for Slieve Gallion, it was already almost 1PM. Luckily, parking is easy in Saint-Pierre and we had been able to find a spot not too far away which had no parking restrictions at all. We ordered a bowl of soup and some croissants. Amy took out her phone and googled the studio address. Nowhere is very far from anywhere else in Saint-Pierre and we were able to set off on foot at 1.45 to arrive in good time.

We were warmly welcomed at the door by Lili who led us up some dusty, wooden stairs and directed us into a tiny walk-in wardrobe that they chose to call their recording studio. She gestured us to sit on two wooden, fold-up chairs that were arranged side by side. Amy chatted to Juliette as I tuned up my guitar. Then Juliette spotted my stool and asked me if she could borrow it. She opened it out and set it in front of where we were seated. She placed a small condenser microphone with three open-out legs on the stool and attached it to her iPhone which she threw onto a small cushion on the floor. I could see that Amy's recording debut already had the makings of a very high-tech event indeed!

After a quick sound check, Juliette sat cross-legged on the cushion and held the iPhone in her hand. We were ready for the countdown to begin.

'OK, allez!' she said and nodded her head. I looked at Amy and then started to strum. Amy began to sing—quite well in the circumstances but not her best. I was beginning to realise that we had stumbled into the world of 'One-Take Studios' and I really wanted Amy to have the chance to do it again. Luckily, Juliette discovered a serious technical glitch (not sure what the problem was but it all sounded very complicated and definitely not Juliette's fault!) so Saint-Pierre Studios prepared itself for that rare thing—a second take. This time the technology didn't fail us and Amy really belted it out with the sort of panache that she had grown into in the market square.

'Would you like to hear it?' Lili asked.

'Yes please!'

Lili plugged a pair of ancient Ear Pods into her phone and handed us an earpiece each. With our heads pressed close together, we listened to the results of the 'final' take. Perfect! Lili and Juliette seemed to be delighted with the end results…even though they had to settle for the fact that it had needed all of two—yes two—takes to finally get there!

Lili turned to Amy. 'Can you do Wednesday in Lisieux? And Pete, can you be there also? We'd be interested in your involvement in this story as well.'

'Of course,' I said, 'I'd be delighted. As long as your listeners can put up with my basic French!'

The young women both laughed. 'Believe me,' Lili said, 'your French is at genius level compared with most of the English visitors we've had!'

She turned back to Amy, the real star of the show.

'And Amy, your French is … so good! It's fantastique!'

Amy smiled, delighted. 'And what time on Wednesday?'

'The broadcast starts at 2 o'clock. There is a mix of popular music and chat and it runs until 3.30PM. But please try to be there by 1PM and we can go through some of the questions we might ask you.'

We said our goodbyes, gave the entire technical crew—well, both of them—a couple of bises each and made our way back to the car and on to Slieve Gallion.

Amy turned to me as we drove home. 'Just got one thing to say to you, guitar boy.'

'Speak to me!'

'Wowzers!' she replied.

27

Annie, Ben and the boys had disappeared by the time we got back. They'd left a note to say that they had gone to the *La Dame Blanche* wildlife conservation centre. This was only about 2 km away from base camp and it was a great favourite destination for the boys!

Amy and I decided on a cup of coffee before we rushed into anything too energetic such as taking a gentle stroll around the village. Waiting for the kettle to boil, I idly glanced at my emails and Amy did the same. Thirty seconds later I said 'Oh my God!' Two seconds later, Amy made the exact same utterance. We looked at each other with concerned expressions.

'You first,' Amy suggested.

'OK then. Well, I haven't bothered you with this before, but …'

Looking rather startled, Amy grabbed my arm. 'Bothered me with what?'

'Oh, please don't panic, Amy. It's nothing terrible! It's just that the university is on a campaign for lazy-arse academics like me to finally get their bloody doctorates over the line.'

'And …?'

'And for my submission they've now confirmed that the absolute deadline has been set for the end of this year.'

'Oh! Can you do it?' Amy asked with concern.

'Yes, I think so. I applied for a sabbatical term to complete it and I'm just waiting to see if the dean will give his approval.'

'And are you hopeful…?'

'Mmm, reasonably. It's in his interest for me to get it done as well as mine, so…I'm just keeping my fingers crossed! Now what about your news?'

Amy looked back at her phone.

138

'Well, it's a long one from Stacey. Do you remember that old bad dude Maurice Charles John, otherwise known as my father? Well, it seems that on Friday he dressed himself in a smart suit, managed to get onto campus and make his way to the faculty building. He must have hung around outside the main entrance and slipped in while someone was leaving. He knocked on a random door and the only person there was a new girl, Chloe, whom I barely know. He got it out of her that I was living with you—she gave him your name, she thinks, but she's not sure of that—and told him that we were living somewhere in Fishermead, but luckily, she didn't know the exact address.'

'What!' I shouted. 'The bugger. We might have known he wouldn't give up that easily!'

Amy nodded. 'We really need to think this through—I don't want him on our tails for the next twenty years!'

'Anyway, I thought the faculty had put out an all-points-bulletin on him,' I added.

'Well, I suppose Chloe didn't get the message,' replied Amy. 'Anyway, it's done and we've just got to hope that he doesn't get any more precise details of where I'm living.'

We both sat in silence for a few moments. Then Amy said 'OK Pete. Let's not let this stand in the way of what we're doing. I refuse to let that man get to me. Agreed?'

'Agreed!' I replied. 'We've got a radio phone-in to prepare for. Such a shame that you'll be stuck sitting beside a guy who can barely speak the language!'

'Oh, you'll be great, as usual, Mister Peter-the-ever-popular. Even if they were to switch to Cantonese half way through, I bet you'd still come out smelling of roses!'

That evening after the boys had gone to bed, we took stock of the situation. Things were moving so quickly for Amy it was hard to keep up. Annie asked her if she felt nervous about the upcoming event in Lisieux. Amy confirmed that the thought had crossed her mind! 'I just can't imagine what sorts of things people will ask,' she said.

We agreed to try a dummy run where the three of us would all fire at her a wide range of questions, both trivial and intrusive, and then she could consider what if anything she might want to say in response. The grilling lasted fifteen minutes. 'Thanks, guys' she said at last. You've no idea how helpful that has been! Now I just have to do in all again but this time entirely in French!'

Ben smiled at Amy encouragingly. 'But the thing is, Amy, your French is perfect. I can't believe that will be a problem for you.'

Amy gave him a wry look. 'That's kind, Ben. Yes, my French is quite good…for a Brit. But when people get excited, as French people often do, they talk so quickly. I still have to work really hard to keep up. The other thing I discovered from this morning is that the local Normandy accent is…wow…it's so very strong—quite different from my audio-books! When people started firing questions at me, it took me a while to tune in.'

'Ha!' I laughed. 'I hear what you're saying! I think if you performed that same gig in Cookstown main street you'd find it every bit as hard to grasp what the locals were asking you.

'Amen to that,' replied Ben. 'I've been there, you know! If it hadn't been for my dear wife here, I don't think I'd have had a clue!'

Annie put her arm around Amy's shoulder. 'Anyway, don't worry, love. My limited experience of these phone-ins is that listeners want to get to know *you* as much as wanting to hear your story. If they like you, they'll care about your message. My advice would be just be yourself and the entire Calvados region of northern France will learn to love you every bit as much as we all do!'

Amy suddenly looked rather emotional.

'Thanks Annie!'

28

Amy and I arrived in good time at the Lisieux studio where we were met and greeted by the production team. Lili and Juliette were now joined by Marcel, the recording engineer. Marcel looked all of sixteen years of age. He was silent and very intense but in the event he handled everything brilliantly, greatly helped by the fact that this trio had run similar events every Wednesday over many months previously.

This time it was Lili who took on the lead role of programme presenter while Juliette donned the headphones and made ready to field the phone calls coming in. In comparison to the facilities in Saint-Pierre, the Lisieux set-up was more like Abbey Road studios! Not only were the chairs soft but the recording equipment looked modern and professionally arranged in a spacious recording booth. Lili's preparation with Amy for the event was minimal but that suited us all. Lili explained that a full recording of the episode would be placed on the website so it would be free for us to access in the future.

Suddenly, on goes the red light and we are '*En Direct*'.

Lili began by outlining the amazing *tumulte* that had taken place in Saint-Pierre-sur-Dîves on Monday morning when a young woman brought the weekly market to a standstill. She described how Amy stood on a kitchen stool and drew a crowd of hundreds of people by singing …this.

Then Marcel faded in the Saint-Pierre studio recording of *Où est ma mère*. Given the circumstances under which it had been made, the sound quality of Amy's voice, in the Lisieux studio at least, was excellent.

Lili continued, 'So, "Where is my mother?" That's the desperate question that has brought Aimée Clotilde Charpentier all the way from the heart of England to visit us here. Calvados was the last place she saw her mother nineteen years ago when she was about 4 years old. And today she's here in the studio with her guitar-playing boyfriend Peter.'

Lili turned to Amy and tossed her a few easy starter questions which Amy handled with aplomb. This was all going much better than I had been expecting. Then she turned to me.

'So, Peter, what has your involvement been in all of this?'

Pow! it was an obvious question but it was just so open-ended that my GCSE French vocabulary simply imploded. After a few embarrassing stammers, Amy leapt to my rescue and restated the question into a form that enabled me to make a few plausible French-sounding grunts. Things rapidly settled down after that and I could see that Amy and Lili were really hitting it off.

Juliette then waved at us to say that the first few calls were starting to come in.

Lili: Our first caller is Eloise, from Orbec. Go ahead with your question, Eloise.

Eloise: (very excited and talking quickly) I was there on Monday in Saint-Pierre. I go every week to the market but... I've never seen anything like it! You were just fantastic. My question is, Are you French or English?

Amy: Thank you for calling, Eloise. Well, I just discovered a few weeks ago that I have a French birth certificate so, "Allez la France", yes, I am French. But I have lived in England since I was about 4 years old.

Eloise: But your French, it is so excellent. I would never have known!

Amy: Thank you so much. Well, I would like it to be good but I still have a lot to learn. You see, I am an only child...at least I think I am... Anyway, I have always read a lot of books in French—Emile Zola, Albert Camus, Simone de Beauvoir. But I often listen to the

142

French ones using audiobooks, which has really, erm … 'learned me to speak proper, like'!

Lili: Ha ha! Thank you for your question, Eloise. So many calls—this is amazing! Our next caller is Josephine from Beuvron-en-Auge. Please go ahead!

Josephine: Hi Aimée. I have two questions. First, did you have a happy home life. And also, who kidnapped you and why?

Amy paused a little before answering.

Lili: Aimée, perhaps these questions are too painful for you…?

Amy: …well … they are painful but I feel I must try to answer them. Thank you, Josephine. Your questions … your questions really go to the, erm, go to the heart of why I am sitting here in a recording studio in beautiful Lisieux. Sadly, I'm not able…actually…I can't remember anything about my time spent with my mother in France. Perhaps if I can meet up with her again, some of those memories will come to the… back to the surface. My last 19 or 20 years living in England with my father have not been happy, no … not happy. [Pause] And the experience made me extremely shy. I became so shy that sometimes, erm, sometimes I could barely speak. My father is English. It was he who stole me away from France, leaving my mother Élise standing waiting for me at the railway station in Lisieux—this very city where I am sitting now. She never…she never saw me again. [Pause] My father told me she was dead but I now think … I now hope … that she is not. [Long pause]

Lili: Just take your time, Aimée.

Amy: Thank you. Well, my mother's name is Élise Camille Charpentier. I recently discovered that fact on my French birth certificate and also that I have been given my *mother's* surname. I am Aimée Clotilde *Charpentier*. In English, Charpentier translates as Carpenter and Carpenter is the name I've been given while in England. But, to my mother…if you are listening to this, Élise, please get in touch. I am desperate to see you and… and… restart our life together!

143

Josephine: Why would your father have done such a thing?

Amy: I'll probably never know why. Perhaps so that I could make his life easier? Perhaps to...how you say... hurt my mother? Or perhaps for some more, erm, virtuous reason? Who knows?

Lili: Thank you, Josephine. Our next caller is Thierry from Pont-l'Évêque. Go ahead, Thierry.

Thierry: First of all, Aimée, welcome home!

Amy: Ha ha! Thank you so much, Thierry!

Thierry: My question is... well let me say that I love your singing! You have a great voice! I'm wondering how long have you been a singer? Where have you performed? Do you write your own songs? Have you made recordings? Or if not, have you any plans to record?

Amy: [laughing] Thank you Thierry for those kind words about my singing. So many questions! But my answer is... well, if only you knew! [turning to me] Can you say something about this, Pete?

Me: Hi Thierry. Well, I just play the...um...the guitar! But Amy's singing has been a big...erm...a big surprise for me...and for her! Truly, until this...seminary, oh no I mean until this *week* we didn't know that Amy could sing so good. As a child...with her father she had...she had not reason to sing. It was to ...send this message to her mother... that gave her reasons to sing. But really...we knew, no I mean we *never* knew what a lovely voice was hiding there! If you can understand what I'm saying!

Thierry: I understand you perfectly! That is amazing! Can I admit an interest here? I work in the music industry. I run a small recording company and we are always looking out for new talent. I do believe that there is a future waiting for you, Aimée. Please don't stop singing!

Amy: Well, that is kind, Thierry. I feel I've just found my voice so perhaps in the future I will find a way to do something with it!

Lili: Thank you, Thierry! Our next caller is Sylvie from here in Lisieux. What's on your mind, Sylvie?

Sylvie: My question is … I would like to ask Aimée … *Pause*.

Amy: Take your time, Sylvie!

Sylvie: Thank you … Aimée. You see, you said earlier that you were shy. Well, I'm shy too. But … but to be honest I would find it easier to …to stick pins in my eyes than stand on a chair in Saint-Pierre-sur-Dîves and … and sing. How could you find the strength to do that?

Amy: Thank you for that question, Sylvie. Yes, in all my life I never would have thought I could do that … but yet I did it. It's funny—since I came to France from England it seems like…it feels like I'm a different person. Like I'm starting over as a new person who's not…constantly…not constantly tied up in knots by nerves and worries!

Sylvie: Oh, I wish I could do that!

Amy: Well, I had a couple of things that helped me. First of all, I had Pete there. I know he really loves me and with him beside me, well, how could I fail? A second reason is that for over 20 years I have been so shy. It's like I've had a… I've had a placard around my neck. But I'm actually getting bored of being "Timid Aimée" all the time so I'm really trying hard to be "Slightly-more-Confident Aimée".

Sylvie: … Maybe Pete has a brother I could borrow for a while?

Amy: Ha ha! Sadly no! But you know, for me, the main reason I could do this performance in Saint-Pierre is that I so much want to find my mother. Pete's mother is from Ireland. She has a saying, that 'faint heart never won fair maid'. Well, I don't want to, you know…to miss out on finding my mother just because I had a faint heart.

Sylvie: Aimée, you are very … inspiring. Thank you!

145

With regular breaks for music, the 90 minutes just flew by. As we approached the final stages, two entertaining calls came through to us.

Odette: Hi Aimée. Bravo! I love you so much. I'd like to say that here in France we all hate our government and we particularly hate our president. Please say that you will come home to Normandy and be our next president. I beg you! *Save* us!

Amy: Ha ha! Thank you, Odette. Wow! The first ever lady president of France? That would be something new…a new direction for me! Perhaps instead I could come back as Queen. How does Queen Aimée the Lionheart sound?

Odette: Ha ha! That sounds perfect. I think you would be the best queen of France ever! I just hope you can avoid the guillotine!

But the star turn was the final caller, Gabriel.

Gabriel: Hello Aimée. My name is Gabriel. I'm a farmer from Liverot, I'm 83 years old and I've never been married.

Lili: Oh, really? And…erm…do you have a question, Gabriel?

Gabriel: My question to Aimée is…I've been waiting for this my whole life. Will you make me the happiest man alive?

Cue general laughter from everyone in the studio. Amy looked at Lili and mouthed, 'What's going on?' Lili, still giggling, whispered back, 'I think he's asking you to marry him!' Once the penny had dropped, Amy grinned back at Lili before returning to the microphone. She took a deep breath.

Amy: Can I ask you two important questions then, Gabriel?

Gabriel: Yes, of course.

Amy: First question. Might the 60 year age gap between us be a problem for you?

Gabriel: Not if it isn't a problem for you!

146

More laughter.

Amy: Ha ha! And my second question. Do you have a cow?

Gabriel: Well, not any more. I sold them all!

Amy: Oh, that's a pity. Unfortunately, I've always promised myself that I'll never marry a man who hasn't got a cow!

At this point I decided to chip in.

Me: Actually, Amy, I don't have a cow!

Loud laughter from Gabriel.

Amy: Well, Pete…this is the first time you've told me that!

Again, there was much snorting laughter to be heard down the line. After a short pause, Amy continued.

Amy: Anyway, Gabriel, I think I'm still much too young to get married. Can you ask me again when I'm, say, 50?

Gabriel: Fifty? But by then I'll be, let me see …'

Me: One hundred and ten, Gabriel!

Amy: Ahh, hurray. The English mathematician saves the day!

There was yet more chortling coming down the phone line from Gabriel. Then he spoke once more but this time in a slower and more serious tone.

Gabriel: Aimée, I'd just like to say that the main thing here is for you to find your mother. I know you will find her because everyone, whatever age they are, needs their mother. What's her name again?

Amy: [slowly] Élise Camille Charpentier.

Gabriel: Well, Élise Charpentier, I hope you are listening. You will be the luckiest mother in the world to discover that you have such a wonderful, resourceful and, erm, talented daughter as Aimée. Good luck, my dear and I hope that everyone listening will really work hard to help you find her … and help her to find you.

I could see Amy starting to well up again.

Amy: [whispered] Thank you so much, Gabriel!

Lili: Yes, thank you Gabriel for that …erm unexpected question. And thank you to the many, many people who phoned in. In all the time that this programme has been running, we've never had such a response. As Gabriel said, Aimée desperately needs to find her mother. Can you help?

Aimée's full name is Aimée Clotilde Charpentier. She is 23 years of age. Her mother's name was Élise Camille Charpentier. She might have remarried so her surname may no longer be Charpentier. How old might she be today? Well, Aimée doesn't know; perhaps between 40 and 65 years. Could she be your neighbour? or your mother? or you? Please phone, send us a message, drop an email onto our website or even write us a letter.

I'm sure all our listeners will agree that Aimée's story has totally captured everyone's heart. She needs to hear from you! Please, please help her to find her mum! I promise you that in the near future we will return to this story and keep you in the loop if anything develops. I leave you with the one key question:

[in English] Where is her mother? [in French] Où est sa mère, Où est sa mère, Où est sa mère, ….

And here, Marcel expertly faded Lili down and dramatically closed the show by once again bringing up the Saint-Pierre studio recording of Amy passionately singing her song, *Où est ma mère*. It was a magnificent *coup de théâtre* and a perfect ending to an unforgettable programme.

148

Merci, Marcel! Merci, Lili! Merci, Juliette!

29

'Hurray! The two famous linguists have returned,' shouted Ben as we wheeled into the back yard of Slieve Gallion.

It was another warm Normandy day. The boys were walking along the mighty River Orbiquet sporting their sun hats but wearing very little else. They spotted us emerging from the car bearing a promising looking *gâteau au chocolat* bought in a Lisieux boulangerie and they immediately became motivated to give us the welcome we felt we deserved!

It didn't take long for two cups of juice and four empty glasses to appear on the white circular table. A chilled bottle of Crémant d'Alsace was popped and we all got stuck into the celebration of Amy's *heure de gloire*.

'We liked the music, Uncle Pete,' said Sam. 'That was the best bit!'

'Sorry—we only grasped bits of the chat,' said Ben. 'Our French is pretty basic I'm afraid!'

Then Annie turned to Amy. 'To be honest, though, Amy, I'm beginning to think our Pete speaks better French than you. I was able to understand every word he said! He speaks it just how I like to hear it—slow, ponderous, stumbling, with a distinct English accent and built around a vocabulary of less than a hundred words!'

'Thanks for that, Annie,' I laughed.

Then Amy put her arm around my waist and said 'You're right. He was brilliant! A toast to Pete, especially for his heroic explanation of my musical awakening, which was *formidable*!'

I stood to take the adulation as everyone toasted me. 'To Peter Campbell, the Cookstown polyglot!'

'Seriously though, Amy,' said Annie, 'what actually happened in that studio?'

Amy quickly ran through some of the key events of the afternoon and everyone particularly enjoyed the tale of Gabriel's marriage proposal.

By now, the boys were taking a great interest in the studio recording story. 'Uncle Pete,' said Sam suddenly, 'are you really going to have to buy a cow now!'

Everyone laughed, particularly Amy.

'And did you get any useful leads at all?' Annie continued.

'Well,' said Amy uncertainly, 'Not yet, but we've set the ball rolling and apparently phone messages and emails are flooding in all the time!'

'So, what's the next step?' Annie continued.

'Well, I asked Marcel the recording engineer this question. I explained to him that we needed to access every message that came in from the listeners. I wanted to know if there was any way that he could let us download them.'

'And what did he say?' asked Ben.

'Well, in true Marcel style, his answer was minimalist. He just nodded and said, "Bon".'

'Did it sound like a good "bon" or a dodgy one?' Ben asked.

'Hmmm. Honestly, I don't know, Ben. Marcel was very hard to read but I have to say that everything he did this afternoon was totally on the money.'

'That's "sur l'argent" in case you're wondering, Annie,' I added, smugly.

'Careful Pete,' replied Annie. 'Don't go overboard!'

'Say, Amy,' said Ben, 'have you had a decent response from your leafletting in Saint-Pierre-sur-Dîves?'

'Well,' replied Amy, 'to date over twenty locals have used the website to send messages of support, which is lovely! I've been checking it every couple of hours but so far nothing of significance has come through.'

'Let's hope the response from this phone-in will bump it up a bit!' said Annie.

151

I was actually quite concerned about Amy getting access to all these messages that listeners were clearly sending in to Radio Calvados. There might never be a second chance. It would be a tragedy if she missed out on these now when any one of them might contain a nugget of information that could make all the difference in her search.

Harry leant on the back of Amy's chair. 'Have you checked your phone? Maybe that Marcel's sent you a message!'

'Good point, Harry!'

She checked her messages and emails. Nothing. I did the same. Still nothing.

Harry wasn't to be defeated. 'What about that new email you made, Uncle Pete? The where-is-my-mother one?'

'No, I haven't checked that one…but I don't think Marcel had that email address.'

'Yes, he did!' said Amy, suddenly. 'I remember giving him one of our leaflets!' In an instant she flipped her phone to access this new email account. Bingo! The eagle had landed! An email message from Marcel had come in just 5 minutes before. Everyone crowded round and Amy translated it!

To Amy and Pete,

There are already 62 messages that have come in from listeners to our station since the programme ended 60 minutes ago. This is unprecedented. I have created a special password-protected folder and copies of all these messages are automatically being sent there. The folder will soon also contain the programme recording and a (French) transcript.

You can access the folder with:

username: **Amy-Pete**

password: **ou-est-elle?**

Good luck with your search, Amy. I hope that next time we meet you will bring us good news about your mother!

Regards, Marcel

A short silence followed Amy's translation.

'What a star!' said Annie.

Both Amy and I were lost for words.

Eventually Amy said, 'I think I seriously underestimated Marcel! First things first—I'm going to email him to say thank you.'

This she did in the twinkling of an eye. Then Amy closed her phone and popped it into her pocket. She looked at me intensely. 'Hey Pete, I think we have a have a big job on for the rest of the evening! Any one of these messages could be her!'

I nodded. 'Yes, it could. Yes, it could!'

30

Amy and I set ourselves up at the kitchen table. She opened up her laptop and accessed the Radio Calvados messages folder.

'Oh my God, Pete, there are over 100 already; 117 to be exact. This is just…unbelievable!' The whole mood was heightened by the fact that, as we began to read through them, the list of messages was continuing to grow.

She was shaking as she started to read out the first few messages. Luckily for me she communicated the contents of each message using my preferred mother tongue! The sentiments expressed by the correspondents were universally positive. Amy's can-do attitude and bravery were much celebrated. But after about twenty or so messages, Amy stopped reading and put her hand on my arm.

'Hang on, Pete. This is lovely and everything. These people are so kind…but…well we have over a hundred to get through and so far…well what do we have to show for it.'

I had to agree with her. 'Hmm, I see what you're saying. I guess the question is—is there anything we've read yet that's got us any closer to finding your mum?'

She shook her head sadly and was by now starting to look quite tearful. Having set out with such very high expectations made this disappointment even harder to bear. I made us a sandwich and a restorative cup of tea, both of which helped us to double down on the task and keep going. It was almost midnight when we decided to call a halt. Out of the 143 messages received, we thought we might have 18 with the potential for useful follow-up.

Next morning, Amy and I set up shop out of doors at the white garden table and began working through the 18 selected messages. In the cold light of day, many of these were starting to look even less promising than they had done the previous evening when excitement levels were still relatively high. We started with the messages that had included an email address and tried to answer each one individually, paying careful attention to the personal details that had been provided.

By mid-morning we had worked through our list. Where phone numbers had been included, Amy made the calls but none of these provided anything remotely promising. Clearly our correspondents had wanted to give us helpful information but the truth was that, for the most part, any information being provided was largely hearsay. By the time Ben joined us with a pot of coffee and a plate of pastries, we were both starting to flag.

'So, how's it going, guys?' Ben asked cheerfully.

Amy, looking white-faced and exhausted managed to offer a weak smile but at first seemed unable to speak. Eventually she replied. 'To be honest, Ben, it's … it's a bit …'

'Slow?' I offered.

'Yes, slow is putting it kindly. Everyone who's responded couldn't have been nicer or more encouraging. They *so* want to help but really, so far, no one knows anything at all about my mum!'

I reached over and squeezed her hand. 'Let's take a break, Aims. I could do with a coffee. And those pastries look so … so very reviving!'

For most of the morning the boys had been dashing around the garden on their bikes. When the pastries were spotted, they came flying in at great speed to join us.

Sam put his arm around Amy's neck. 'Have you found her yet?' he asked.

'No, not yet Sam but we're not giving up. Remember what old Gabriel said!'

'Yup,' responded Harry, 'I remember. He said … um … everyone needs their mother!' He walked around the table and gave

155

Annie a big sloppy kiss on the cheek. Sam immediately followed suit.

'Thanks boys!' said Annie, looking genuinely surprised but also delighted, if not a bit misty-eyed. 'And never you forget it!' she added, emphatically.

Suddenly "ping" went my phone. I glanced at the screen. 'Oh, this one's from the dean of the faculty! I'd better, you know…' I went inside to the kitchen in order to give it my full attention.

Ten minutes later I rejoined the rest of the family in the garden. 'Everything OK, Pete?' Amy asked with some concern. I nodded. 'Yes, fine. Everything's fine. In fact, it's very fine. It was about my application for sabbatical leave to complete my thesis.'

Amy's eyes widened. 'And…?'

'Well, it's really good news. I've been given four months to get it done!'

Amy jumped out of her chair and gave me a huge hug. 'That's just great, Pete…you jammy bugger!'

Ben looked a bit confused. 'So, when you say sabbatical leave do you mean *paid* leave?'

I couldn't suppress my elation and nodded enthusiastically. 'My God!' said Ben. 'I like the sound of that. I might take some sabbatical leave and write a paper on, mmm let me see…what's my area of specialism, I wonder? The art of digging with a spade, I think!'

'I'm sure your thesis will be ground-breaking, love!' Annie snapped back. Ben grinned. 'Back-breaking, more like!' Everyone laughed. Both Annie and Ben gave me the thumbs up. 'Well done, little brother!' 'Yea, well done, mate!'

Amy was still looking concerned. 'So, when does the period of leave begin?'

'Pretty much as soon as I can get all the admin ducks in a row. When we're back, I'll be getting straight onto it.'

That evening, just after the boys had retired to bed, Ben turned to Amy. 'So, going back to your mum, Amy, what's happened with all the other avenues of enquiry. Has anything come of them at all?'

Amy looked thoughtful. 'Well, the truth is, Ben, not much. Not much at all, I'm afraid.'

'But what about the DNA search? Do you not have hopes there?'

Amy shook her head. 'I'm hoping to take a DNA test next week so at least I'll soon exist on various DNA databases waiting for someone to find me. Loads of people in America and the UK have done the same so our overall database is huge. That's just not the case in other countries.'

'Not even in France?' Ben asked.

'Particularly not in France, apparently! I've been googling that last week and it turns out that it's illegal to take a paternity DNA test in France.'

Ben looked appalled. 'You're kidding! Could you maybe get around it by sending someone in France a test kit from the UK?'

'Probably,' Amy replied. 'In fact, this was what was suggested to me by a very nice woman I talked to from one of the heritage sites. But ... well I dug a bit deeper and if you get caught doing this, it could be punishable by a €15,000 fine or even up to a year in prison!'

'Whaaaaat??' Annie said. 'That's so harsh. Why would they do that?'

Amy smiled ruefully. 'They have a very different way of looking at it over here. I've made a note about it.' Amy leafed through her green notebook. 'Ah, here it is. Apparently, it's all about "upholding the French regime of filiation and preserving the peace of families".'

Annie looked shocked. 'What's *filiation*, when it's at home?'

'... it means, erm ... a child being designated to a particular parent or set of parents.'

Annie looked outraged. 'Hmmph! I don't know about preserving the peace of families ... more like preserving the place of patriarchy, I'd say!'

Amy shrugged. 'No, I don't like it but I've just got to take it or leave it! But I feel I've tried all the obvious things. I've even filled

157

in forms with the Red Cross. But if Élise Camille Charpentier is living in Normandy, she's keeping her head firmly down. Assuming she's still alive, of course.'

I put my arm around Amy's shoulder and kissed her on the cheek. 'Don't worry, Amy. We've no reason to believe she's not alive. You'll get there—I know you will.'

Amy's eyes started to fill with tears as she shook her head. 'But we've got nowhere, Pete! All this singing and...the broadcast and the messages and everything. It's been great fun but what have they actually achieved?'

I had to agree with her. The answer was, so far not much. Annie gave Amy a sympathetic look. 'The thing to remember, though, is that you've made a start. There are now hundreds of people in Normandy who have heard the story of Élise Charpentier and know about her daughter's quest to find her. People talk to people who talk to people and so it goes round. But this all takes time. Look, you've lots going for you. You speak the language and, haven't you got the wonder boy here to help you!'

Amy smiled in return. 'I'm so grateful for your support. Thanks all of you. It means so much that I'm not doing this on my own. I suppose what I'm feeling at the moment is that here I am in Normandy searching for my mum and...well, I just haven't a clue where to start looking! Before I know it I'll be back in Milton Keynes and thinking I just wasted a big opportunity!'

There was a silence in the room as tears began to flow down Amy's cheeks. I put my arm around her shoulder once more. 'I'm going to make you a promise, Aims. This is your first visit to Normandy but it will not be the last. We're going to come back and next time we'll be really well organised in advance.'

Amy smiled. 'When?' she asked.

'Soon. Very soon. I promise! But for now, let's think about it a different way. Annie's right—you've started the ball rolling with the broadcast and we need to be patient. That might well lead somewhere next week or next month—who knows? But in the meantime, we've got three more days here so let's not waste them. This region is where your mum once lived and breathed. I've got my

158

car. Why don't we just explore it. We can visit the sorts of places that she may have once visited and…oh I don't know… let's just breathe in the atmosphere of the world she once lived in.'

To my relief she nodded enthusiastically. We spent the next hour looking at a map of the region and exploring possible locations for a visit, starting with the city of Lisieux.

I filled and switched on the kettle and then popped out to the loo. Coming back through the hall I spotted a little painting on the wall that had fond memories for me. Thinking it might lighten the mood, I took it off its hook and returned with it to the sitting room where four coffee cups and some slices of gateau had magically appeared. I held the art-work up for all to see and smiled at Annie. 'I can't believe you painted this when you were twelve!' She laughed. 'What was it you used to call it? Oh yes, the recumbent walrus, that was it.'

Amy twisted her head to get a better look. 'So, what is it exactly?'

Annie laughed. 'What do *you* think it is?'

'Mmm. I'm guessing maybe a sleeping animal—could be a seal or a bull, perhaps?'

Ben smiled, 'Oh don't be put off by that walrus thing. I can tell you it's not an animal!'

Amy scratched her head for a few moments. 'I give up. What is it?'

'OK,' said Annie, who I knew was secretly pleased to revisit her artistic masterpiece for the benefit of her nearest and dearest family members. 'This is Slieve Gallion, the mountain that we could see from our kitchen window in Cookstown.'

'Ahhh!' said Amy. 'I get it. And now it's pride of place in…Slieve Gallion!'

Annie nodded. 'Yea, Slieve Gallion is part of a range known as the Sperrin mountains. It is actually in County Derry but it's so close to County Tyrone that we could see it clearly in Cookstown. I remember it was purple in winter and a sort of greenish brown in the summer. Mum and dad have always said that its shape is burned forever into their subconscious brains.'

159

'Have you climbed it?' asked Amy.

'Yes,' I replied. 'When Annie and I were teenagers, the four of us managed to get all the way up.'

Annie continued, 'It's just over 500 metres so not huge but we were well and truly knackered by the time we got to the top.'

'And magnificent views of County Derry, no doubt?' asked Amy.

Annie and I both laughed. 'Not a sausage!' she replied. 'I remember moaning like hell all the way up! Mum kept saying, "Oh it'll be worth it!" By the time we'd got to the top, the mist and rain had swept in and we had to beat a retreat.'

Ben made a face. 'Mist and rain in Ireland? Whatever next!'

Annie smiled, enjoying the reminiscence. 'But we weren't to be defeated. Ten years later we all went back to have another go. By then it was too much for dad's dodgy knees but we were able to take the car all the way to the summit!'

Amy gave a thumbs up. 'And …?'

'And…success. This time the views were just spectacular. We could practically see the whole of Ulster. Mum and dad knew every village and townland and we spent a good hour looking for recognisable landmarks.'

'Yes,' I continued. 'I remember we could see Donegal to the west. To the north-east we could just make out the Hills of Islay in Scotland. And of course, mighty Lough Neagh stretched out like a monstrous magical blue carpet to the south east.'

'And from one vantage point we could see Lough Fea,' Annie added. 'It's just outside Cookstown. Fabulous! I remember mum saying that it used to freeze over a lot in the winter and her dad, with another group of lads, once drove his Austin 7 across the ice.'

Ben's eyes widened. 'Oops. Don't listen to this, kids. Health and Safety alert!'

There was a short silence as everyone tried to imagine the scene.

Then Amy tugged my sleeve and whispered, 'We could go to Slieve Gallion, Pete.'

'We could,' I replied. 'Some day we will.'

31

Back home again to Blighty I had much to do in preparation for my period of study leave. The various university courses that I chaired needed to be allocated to one or more safe pairs of hands for the duration of my absence. Luckily all my courses were under the care of a couple of excellent course managers who were very experienced and totally on top of the admin side of things. I was able to co-opt the services of two colleagues who agreed to handle any simple academic issues arising, with the proviso that I would be available on email if anything out of the ordinary cropped up. And of course, Stacey was there to oversee things — on past experience I knew that there wasn't much that she couldn't sort out efficiently and with very little fuss.

While we'd been away in France, Amy had started to receive emails from her dad. She refused to read them and blocked his contact details so that they ended up in her junk folder. This seemed to me to be a very sensible course of action as I felt that the less contact she had with him the better. So, it was something of a surprise when she said one evening 'Hey Pete, I was thinking … um … I might make contact with my dad again.'

Needless to say, I felt I had to perform a few shaky staggers, before collapsing theatrically onto the sofa.

'All right, all right, you big poser!' Amy laughed. 'I know this is a bit of a change of direction but I, … well, I've been thinking …!'

I straightened up in the chair and asked 'So … why?'

'There are several reasons. First, I'm certain that he knows some stuff that I'd like to hear about. To be honest, we haven't really made any progress with finding my mum and he's too good a source of information to give up on. Second, we'll be over there again soon…'

I nodded slowly. 'Well, soonish!'

'Soon! You definitely said soon, Pete. Remember!'

'Oh, alright then. Let's say soon!'

'The point is, if I'm ever going to get information out of him then this is the time to do it.'

I nodded again.

'And also … well you'll probably think I'm mad but …' Amy paused and seemed to be unable to continue.

'Look Amy, you're never mad! Remember my good friend Monsieur Blaise Pascal. Sometimes the heart knows what the mind knows not of!'

Amy walked across to the sofa, put her arms around my neck and snuggled up tight against me.

'OK, the third thing is that…over the last ten days my dad has written me six emails. I decided to have a look at them. If I believe what he's saying, … and I'm still not totally convinced … there are some indications of regret and, maybe even a wish to try to make it right.'

We sat quietly for a few moments. This was something of a bombshell for both of us. Then Amy said, 'Come on, Pete. Talk to me!'

'OK then. I have to admit that my immediate reaction was thinking how much I actually hate this man who was such a cruel bully and so really horrible to you.'

I paused for a moment to organise my thoughts.

'OK,' she said slowly. 'And your more…your more considered reaction is …?'

'Well, it's this. What you're saying makes sense. Provided you can be in his company without being physically sick on the carpet, there are things to be gained by meeting up with him. So … I'd support you in any way I could!'

Amy kissed me on the cheek. 'Good old Pete! Ever the support! As I was just saying to the dean at the exam board meeting recently, when it comes to support, Pete's better than a 40-inch D cup any day of the week!'

We both laughed at this uplifting scenario.

'Actually, Pete, there is a fourth thing. Being with you guys in France last week made me think a lot about what it means to be part of a family. At the end of the day, he is my father … well, I think he is. But I don't want to be one of those people who spend their life not speaking to other members of their family. I really don't want that, even when they've behaved very badly.'

I kissed her hand. 'Well said! A bend in the road isn't the end of the road.'

The following afternoon I was in my office having a planning meeting with Stacey—well, more of an informal conversation about what the next four months might look like. When we'd finished the admin side of things, Stacey suddenly said 'Oh Pete, there was something else I wanted to chat to you about.'

'Oh, yes?'

'It's about Amy. She's just asked me if she can take another three weeks leave!'

I blinked in surprise.

'So, you know nothing about this, then?'

'No, I don't. This is news to me.'

'Well, I don't want to create a domestic but… this is awkward for me just now. I'm sure you've noticed that Janice is about to "pop"—she'll be on maternity leave in a couple of weeks. Jade will be leaving us in October. We're already down on secretarial support and it's going to get a whole lot worse. So…I'm starting to panic. I can't do it all on my own!'

I patted Stacey's arm. 'Mmm, I can see that, Stace. I don't know what to say until I've spoken to Amy. All I can tell you is that she's burning up with trying to find her mum at the moment.'

Stacey nodded. '…oh, I know that. I can see how much it all means to her. But…you know…'

'I'll have a word, Stacey. Let's see if we can all work out something between us that satisfies everyone.'

163

An hour later, Amy was sitting with me in the coffee bar. 'Everything all right, Aims?' I asked. She nodded slowly. 'Yes, I think so. Why are you asking?'

I told her briefly about the conversation I'd just had with Stacey. Amy looked slightly shocked and put her hand over her mouth. 'Oh no! I think she got slightly the wrong end of the stick there.'

'What do you mean?'

'Well, I really wasn't making a formal request for three weeks leave or *anything* like that. I just happened to mention that I wanted to go back soon to continue my search for my mother. She asked how long for and I just said I didn't know but ideally for up to two or three weeks. I'd no idea she would see it as more than that. How awful! I feel dreadful now if she thinks I'm being…disloyal.'

'How much of your annual leave have you left, by the way?'

'I have one more week this year. Anything more and I'd have to apply for unpaid leave.'

'Hmm, well, I suppose that might work, but I think from Stacey's point of view, two weeks is more realistic than three.'

'Oh, I'd settle for that!'

'Now, on a point of information, Ms Carpenter, were you planning to embark on this next Normandy adventure on your own or might it involve me at all?'

Amy reddened. 'Oh Pete! I know I should have talked it over with you first but…well *of course* it will involve you. We always planned to go back together—remember!'

Amy was clearly still nervous that she had spoken out of turn to Stacey.

'So, Pete, was Stacey very upset with me, then?'

'Just panicking, I'd say. She's losing Janice and Jade over the next few weeks so she's, you know…a bit nervous about coping with everything if you're talking about taking time off too.'

Amy looked thoughtful. 'Well, the staff shortage won't really kick in 'til the end of September. So as long as I'm back before Janice leaves on maternity leave…and you and I did agree on *soon* rather than *soonish, so*…!'

'Ah yes, I do remember you squeezing that promise out of me! OK then, here's my proposal. I can just as easily work on my thesis in France, so that's not a problem. Let's try to get back to Normandy as soon as we can realistically arrange it. We'll stay for two weeks and be back in good time to satisfy Stacey's staffing worries.'

Amy clapped her hands in excitement. 'Oh, thanks Pete. I just can't wait! When shall we go?'

'Oh, I'd say…soonish! Er, sorry, I mean soon!'

32

The following evening, we were sitting in the Swan Inn, awaiting the arrival of Maurice. Amy, not surprisingly, hadn't wanted to return to the family home for this potentially tricky encounter and so she'd agreed to meet him on neutral ground. She fished out the green notebook from her bag and started to look through the few list points that she'd already made. Maurice joined us a couple of minutes after we arrived. He looked as if he'd washed and shaved for the occasion and was wearing the dark suit that was now the stuff of sartorial legend in the faculty.

What now, I wondered? First off, we needed to get through a few dicey moments of greeting etiquette — to kiss? (deffo not!), to hug? (nope), to shake hands? (possibly) or to nod to each other in a stiff, awkward male manner (probably) … all very delicate.

'Hello dad,' Amy said, quietly.

'Hello, love. Are you alright?'

Amy nodded. 'Dad, this is Pete.' I reached out and shook his hand. He looked me in the eye and nodded 'Pleased to meet you, Pete.'

I took their drinks orders and headed for the bar. There was quite a queue, so I had the chance to look back at my two drinking companions seated awkwardly facing each other at the table. Amy had her arms folded in front of her and seemed to be staring down at her feet. Maurice's gaze was directed more at the empty pool table. But whatever way they chose to look, it didn't seem to be in the direction of each other. Eventually I returned with the drinks on a tray. Maurice took a sip and cleared his throat. We were off to a flying start!

Amy looked nervously at Maurice. 'So, dad, how've you been keeping?'

'Oh, you know, OK I suppose.'

'Getting your shopping done OK?'

Maurice nodded.

'And your meals? everything…good there?'

'Yes, that's been…you know, fine. What about yourself?

Amy nodded. 'Good, yea, good.'

This was followed by an uncomfortably long silence. Jesus Christ, when was this show actually going to kick off? I said nothing, hoping that natural forces would win out. Eventually they did and surprisingly, it was Maurice who broke the impasse.

'Er, thanks … thanks for agreeing to meet me, Amy,' he began. 'I really … erm … appreciate it.'

Amy's sense of empathy and good manners would normally be kicking in at this point with some sort of response that was a little encouraging. But she didn't.

'The main thing I wanted to say, Amy …,' he began. He swallowed and looked up to the low ceiling of the pub, searching for inspiration. 'The main thing is, I'm sorry.'

Amy raised her eyebrows but still said nothing. Maurice searched her face for a response but found none.

'I treated your mother badly—I know I did— and then…I did the same to you. Well, here I am, getting older and sitting on my own at night staring…staring at the TV.'

Still silence from Amy.

Maurice looked across at me and then back at her.

'Are you … happy, Amy?'

This question seemed to unblock Amy's resistance. She looked over at me and then back at Maurice. She even managed a scintilla of a smile. 'Yes, dad. I really couldn't be happier!'

Maurice's face suddenly relaxed a touch. 'I'm so glad. You're a good girl … and you deserve to be, you know …'

He paused as if searching for the word.

'… loved!' I completed the sentence for him.

'Yes,' Maurice nodded slowly. 'Loved. I'm so sorry that I couldn't, you know …' He paused, again unable to complete his sentence. I filled the silence.

'Well, Maurice, I hope you'll be pleased to know that Amy *is* loved now. Very much!'

Maurice nodded but again no words emerged. After a few seconds, a tear appeared at the corner of his eye. He wiped it away with the back of his hand. Amy and I shared a glance and our eyes both widened. So, the old bastard had a heart after all. Amy was then able to find the composure to open a conversation with him that she had never managed to do in all the 23 years she had known him.

'Well, dad, I suppose you must care about me a bit… or you wouldn't be sitting here now. But I've got some big questions that I need answers to. Can you tell me truthfully?'

Maurice looked very uncomfortable. He took out a tissue, blew his nose and nodded.

'I'll do my best then,' he replied.

Amy glanced at her notebook. 'First question. Are you really my dad?'

'Yes, I promise you that I am.'

Amy paused to take a deep breath. 'OK. You told me that my mum was dead. Is that true?'

Maurice shifted uncomfortably in his chair. Eventually he said 'No… well, I can't say for certain…'

'What's that supposed to mean? As far as you know, is she still alive and living in France?'

'Well, yes, probably.'

'And have you heard from her since you left?'

'Er, no. I don't think…I haven't talked to her since I left with you, no.'

'But have you *heard* from her since you left? Not even a letter?'

Maurice shook his head. 'No, nothing.'

Amy suddenly looked very cross. 'Dad, you promised you'd be truthful! You haven't made a very good start. I happen to know there was a letter in your bedroom drawer from her, written after you left with me.'

Now it was Maurice's turn to look cross. 'You should never have taken those things! And there's still stuff of mine you took that I want back!'

'Never mind that!' Amy replied firmly. 'I want to know how you got that letter. How did she know where to send it to?'

Maurice wrinkled his brow, apparently trying to refresh his memory. 'Oh, *that* letter. I remember it now. It went to a mate of mine—he passed it on to me.'

Amy shot me a glance and raised her eyebrows. I shrugged. 'So did you reply to that letter then?'

'No, no. I just wanted a clean break.'

Amy took a moment to process these bombshells. Then she asked, 'How old was I when we left … when you took me from her?'

Maurice pondered the question. 'Very young. About three, I think.'

'And that's when you brought me back to England?'

He nodded.

I'd resolved to leave the interview in Amy's capable hands but I just couldn't stop myself.

'But *why*, Maurice? Why did you do it?'

Maurice sat silent and miserable, slowly shaking his head. Eventually he said, 'I don't know. I was angry, I suppose. But the main thing was she was about to take Amy away from me and I couldn't bear that.'

He turned back to address Amy.

'You see … in order to get you back to England, I had to smuggle you out illegally. So, for the last 20 years I've been, you know … thinking they'd be coming after me.'

'They?' asked Amy. 'Who are they?'

Maurice had suddenly aged ten years. He only managed to shake his head. 'I don't know. I don't know.'

I could now see him as a rather pathetic old man who didn't really know who he was or why he'd made the life choices that he had made. If he hadn't been the old bastard who'd nearly ruined Amy's life, I could almost have felt sorry for him.

Amy took another look at her notebook.

'How old would mum be now?'

Maurice closed his eyes and seemed to be lost in his thoughts. He shook his head 'No, I can't remember. It was all too…'

'…Come on dad. Think! These things really matter to me!'

He closed his eyes again. 'I'd say she was, um, 23 when I left so now, she'd be … um, 43 I suppose.'

Amy looked away. 'Just my age—oh God!' she whispered.

'And where did we live in France?'

'In the north part.'

'Would that be Normandy?' I asked.

Maurice shrugged 'I suppose.'

'Can you remember any particular places?' Amy continued.

Maurice shook his head. 'It was a very long time ago… We moved around a bit. One place I remember was near the sea…' He rubbed his forehead as if trying to revitalise the brain cells.

'Dieppe?' I suggested.

He shook his head.

'Was it a city or a smaller town?'

Silence.

'But definitely by the sea?'

'Yes, by the sea. Pretty little place. Lots of boats.'

'Deauville? Renville? Honfleur…?'

'That could be it. Honfleur rings a bell. I liked it there. Yes, I think we spent some time in Honfleur … then we moved to a city—Rouen was it, and then… a tiny village in the country—I can't remember the name of that place.'

He paused, lost in thoughts about his now long distant French adventure. Amy continued.

'Do you have a photo of her?'

'No, I never kept any photos from France. I think I burnt them all.'

'Did she have family—parents, brothers and sisters?'

'She never talked about that.'

'And what about our names? I asked you about this when I was little but I never got a proper answer. Why do I have my mother's name?'

170

Maurice considered the question carefully.

'Well, that was very complicated.' He paused once more. 'You need to understand that your mother and me…well we had quite an …up-and-down relationship. During the time that she was expecting you…well, we weren't getting along. Things eventually got so bad that she kicked me out. I came back to England for three or four months. But, fair play, she contacted me a few weeks after you were born to tell me the good news.'

'Was it good news dad?'

Maurice stared intently into Amy's face and for the first time that evening his face lit up with a genuine smile. 'I just can't tell you how much! I was over the moon about it. I really loved you Amy. I know I'm not good at showing it, but…I still do.'

Amy looked away to compose herself. After a long pause she turned back to face him.

'But that doesn't explain the name difference.'

'No, no. Anyway after a few friendly phone calls we agreed to try again. So, I went back. Of course, by then she'd already completed all the paperwork and given you her name.'

'But her name isn't Carpenter. It's Charpentier, the French spelling. And while we're at it, what happened to Aimée and my middle name, Clotilde?'

Once again, Maurice started to look uneasy. 'Yes, well I just thought you'd get on better in England with…with an English-sounding name. There are lots of Carpenters over here but I've never met a Charpentier.'

There was a short silence as Amy and I processed this version of Amy's history. I decided to chip in.

'Well, that was thoughtful of you Maurice. And I would possibly have believed you except that when I look at your own surname you seem to be using John but on Amy's birth certificate you're down as Johns, with an 's'.

By now Maurice was starting to look distinctly queasy. He took a long gulp of his beer. 'Oh, that must have been Élise. I wasn't there when she filled in the forms and it was probably just a slip. She must …'

'…Sorry dad,' interrupted Amy, now looking quite cross. 'I've also seen your passport and your birth certificate. You're down there as Johns as well. But whenever you sign anything or introduce yourself you use Maurice John. In all the time we've lived together in England you've never used Johns.'

Maurice shook his head slowly. 'Well, I can't really explain that. As I said, I wasn't there when that form was filled in, so…'

Amy was now starting to raise her voice. 'While we're on the subject of names, dad,' Amy interrupted, 'when you decided to change my name to something English, why did you not just call me the same name as you were using—the name John? That's always been a problem for me at school. People kept asking me why I didn't have your name and I could never give a proper answer because you would never tell me!'

This was followed by a very long silence. Eventually he spoke. 'Yes, I should have done that really. I think I wanted to keep both names…' He quickly corrected himself, '…I mean, your name, *your* name as similar as possible to what was on your French birth certificate. Just in case, you know, just in case…'

It seemed that this particular line of enquiry had run out of steam, so Amy moved things on with another question.

'OK. Let's not talk about that any more. Tell me, what was my mum like?'

Maurice stared intently into Amy's face. 'She was lovely. She looked a lot like you. She was kind…she would have done anything for anybody. She used to sing, did Élise. Around the house, you know. She had a good singing voice. Sometimes she would sing at the Karaoke. Brought the house down, she did!'

Amy face was suddenly drained of colour. Quite abruptly, she stood up and put her bag on her shoulder. 'I have to stop now,' she said, suddenly. 'Thanks for the chat, dad. Better late than never, I suppose.'

Maurice looked shocked at her sudden change of mood. 'No, don't go, don't go, love. Please! Let's not part like this. Let's talk about something else…'

172

Nothing was forthcoming from Amy in response to this suggestion.

For the first time that evening, he turned to me. 'So, Pete, what is it you do?'

'I work at the university—maths department.'

'Oh, that must be a good job then. I was never any good at maths myself. Never could see the point of it.'

I stared back at him in silence. Amy certainly hadn't come to this important meeting with her dad to discuss either his or my love of mathematics. He turned back to his daughter once more.

'Oh Amy, you know that landlord of ours. What a pompous young… Anyway, he keeps getting onto me asking for the rent. Bloody cheek. He says we're two months behind. Well, I know that can't be right. I gave him a right earful last time, so I'm hoping he won't be back in a hurry…'

Amy gave him a cold stare. She sat down again. After a long pause she said 'Is that the real reason you're here, dad? You want me to pay the rent.'

'No no, I promise you it's not, love. It's…you see, I've got two big jobs on just now and I'm waiting to…you know…get paid.'

Amy continued to stare at him silently.

I decided to press him on this. 'What jobs, Maurice? What exactly do you do?'

He looked at me with a half-smile but I sensed a deep resentment simmering beneath the surface.

'Oh deliveries…special deliveries.'

'So, what sort of special deliveries?'

'Oh, specialist equipment and…that sort of thing—items that wouldn't travel well with a normal carrier.' Amy took over. 'Specialist equipment, dad. Seriously? In your grubby little blue van? It looks to be more suitable for transporting, say, live animals than specialist equipment.'

Maurice looked startled at this comment but said nothing in return. Then his demeanour changed and suddenly he adopted a conciliatory tone.

'You see, Amy, when I had that terrible illness four years ago I just couldn't… I just couldn't do a normal job any more. Then when I was told that I might not be around for much longer I was…desperate to get you settled into a job so you'd be able to look out for yourself after I was gone. I was really thinking of you, love.'

He gazed affectionately at his daughter and then gave her a loving father's concerned smile.

Amy stared back at him and shook her head. 'That's bullshit and you know it, dad. I've seen the letter from the doctor. "Mild alcoholic poisoning", it said. Well, you seem to have made a miraculous recovery from that!'

Now it was Maurice's turn to show anger. 'You don't know what you're talking about girl. You've no idea what I've been through. Anyway, when it comes to…falsifying…documents, you want to be careful yourself. I'd only have to have a word with your employer and you'd be out through the front door of that university quick as wink and you wouldn't have time to collect your coat on the way out!'

I knew that Amy really loved her job and would have been very stung by this threat. I was infuriated by his cheap attempt to intimidate her and looked Maurice hard in the face.

'Really Maurice, is that the best you've got? Do you think anybody in the university will give two hoots about possible irregularities in Amy's paperwork from two jobs back. She got a fantastic reference from her last employer and she's brilliant at her job now. I think you should look a bit closer to home when it comes to breaking the law. We know exactly what you and Jimbo have been up to and it's being going on for years. We know all about this "specialist equipment" that you've been "handling". You'd be "barking mad" if you think we don't. We know Jimbo creates the false documentation for your stolen "cargo". So don't you *dare* threaten Amy, because it could end very badly for you!'

Well, this was the text of the verbal attack running around my head that I was ready to launch. But in reality, I chose to remain silent and leave the response to Amy. Eventually she spoke once more but this time with a calm measured response. 'I think it's time

174

you got yourself a real job, dad. A job that's legal and pays you properly. And if you can't find one, then just sign on and the benefit office will have to pay your rent.'

Still nothing from Maurice. Eventually Amy said 'OK dad, I get it. You can't pay the rent. Here's what I'm going to do. I'll arrange a bank transfer and I'll pay one month. You don't need to pay me back. But that's it. No more!'

She headed for the door. I picked up my phone and keys and followed behind her. We got into the car and Amy sat in silence all the way home.

33

Amy lay curled up beside me on the sofa. Tears streaked her face. 'That was hard, Aims. It must have been painful for you.'

Amy looked away into the far distance and then intensely back at me. She nodded.

'Would you like to talk about it?' I asked her.

'Not yet,' she replied, slowly. 'Maybe in a bit.'

I made us a coffee and we shared one of her brownies. As the sugar kick started to bite, traces of the old Amy began to resurface.

'Thanks. I feel a bit better, actually.' She was ready to talk about what had just happened. 'You know Pete, I'm so glad you were there. I don't think I could have pulled that off on my own.'

'Well, as a matter of fact, Aims, you pretty much did! One thing though. What did you make of the name change from Johns to John? That was one bit of the conversation where I didn't believe him. I can't buy the story it was just a slip of the pen.'

'No,' said Amy slowly, 'he really had no answer to that. But I think I know why he did it.'

I raised my eyebrows as she continued. 'He admitted that by taking me away from my mother against her will and smuggling me illegally out of France, he'd broken the law. He knew it was likely that my mother would have come looking for me in England. But he also knew that, if he and I both had new names, she would have trouble tracking me down. So…he changed both our names, but he altered them just a little bit to make it look like a slip of the pen.'

I took her hand and kissed it. 'You might just be right there. That may have explained why he spent the last twenty years on the move, constantly looking over his shoulder and always living on the edge.

But that thing at the end, asking you for the rent. That was a real kick in the nuts!'

Amy nodded. 'Well…that's the man he is. But as a matter of fact, I don't care so much about the money. What really upset me was hearing something about what my mother was like as a person. I don't remember her, Pete, but I so miss her. I so miss her. I can't stop thinking about…oh the lost years. The two of us spending time together—simple things like doing a job in the kitchen, maybe cooking a meal and…and singing together. It's heartbreaking!' I held her tightly.

We spent a long time in silence. Eventually, and to my considerable surprise, she suddenly started to giggle. I looked at her querulously. 'Was it something I said?'

'No. Not at all. I don't really know why I'm laughing. Just put it down to…nervous hysteria with a dash of post-traumatic stress!

'Well, I'm taking that as a good thing, then.'

She smiled. 'To be honest, Pete, it's beginning to feel like a great weight has been lifted off. I'd no idea how much it was all dragging me down until now!'

I kissed her solemnly on the forehead.

Suddenly we both jumped when Amy's phone pinged and then pinged again a few seconds later.

She picked it up and her eyes widened.

'Hey, two text messages—both from France. How intriguing is that! This one's from Marcel, the sound engineer from Lisieux studio.'

I nodded.

'OK, pin back your ears, Pierre. Here's the English translation.

Dear Aimée,

I hope you are well. Have you had any news of your mother? We've had nothing yet, unfortunately. You told me that you and your boyfriend were planning to return to Normandy soon. We (Radio Calvados) would like to broadcast a short follow-up feature on your story very soon—perhaps in two or three weeks' time. To give it an extra frisson of excitement we hope there will be a special twist to the broadcast. You may remember that one of the callers to your phone-in was called Thierry and he runs a recording studio. He and I are quite good friends and he has a plan for you. I'll let him tell you about it himself.

See you soon, I hope,

Marcel Martin, Radio Calvados, Lisieux

Amy and I exchanged significant glances!

'Read on, madame!' I said encouragingly. 'You're getting me very excited now!'

'OK, then. This one's from Thierry Thomas, *Gardez-le-Local* Recording Studio, Pont-l'Évêque.'

Dear Aimée,

Do you remember me? I will certainly not forget your voice! I really meant it when I invited you to make a recording at my studio in Pont-l'Évêque. I hope that your boyfriend will be able to accompany you on his guitar. If you need further instrumentation, we can also help with that. Any musical genre that you choose will be fine with me!

You may already have heard from my friend Marcel. Our idea is that you record something fabulous and then we use this recording to introduce the piece that Radio Calvados have planned for you. Please say yes. It may help in your quest for où-est-ma-mère. But even if it doesn't, it would be at worst a keepsake for you and at best, the start of something big! I think, I hope, the second of these!

Very best wishes,

Thierry Thomas, Gardez-le-Local Recording Studio, Pont-l'Évêque.

Amy mouthed to me an intense silent scream.

178

I put my arms around her and gave her a short kiss on each cheek and a longer one on the lips.

'Oh, Amy. This is just so …!'

'I know!' she replied. 'It's just so amazing …!'

'One thing that's in our favour. The timing might work well as far as Stacey's staffing worries are concerned.'

Amy grinned delightedly. 'Yes, I'll get straight onto Marcel and Thierry and nail down some definite dates. I'll insist on *soon* rather than *soonish*, of course!'

'Good plan! So, what do you think you might sing in Thierry's studio?'

'I have absolutely no idea!'

'Hmm. I've just had a thought. Can I play it for you?'

She nodded enthusiastically.

I picked up my guitar and started to play, slowly, the chords of the song that I'd been working on while she had taken the bus ride to say goodbye to her father— the old sixties classic, *How Insensitive.*

Suddenly Amy said, 'Hey Pete, that was one of *your* Top 25 playlist tunes.'

Quite soon, Amy started humming along. When I'd finished, she looked at me with a massive grin.

'That was … really, … I just love that song! Astrud Gilberto?'

I nodded. 'It's called *How Insensitive*.'

'Those chords are … so scrummy. Well, aren't you clever, Mr Guitar Pete!'

Amy fished out her phone and quickly found the lyrics to the song. 'Play it again, if you please.'

This time she sang along. It was gorgeous and the song suited her voice perfectly.

'Well,' I said to her. 'I think you might have just found your song for Thierry.'

Amy nodded slowly. 'I think I might!'

34

Well, Thierry was certainly a man of his word. With the deadline of the radio transmission looming, he was anxious to crack on with the recording. Forty-eight hours after we'd returned to Slieve Gallion, he had us over to his studio in Pont-l'Évêque—just for a chat. Clearly, he was looking forward to the prospect of recording Amy's voice the following day.

'So, Aimée,' he asked excitedly. 'What musical treat do you have for us tomorrow?'

'It's a little Bossa Nova number that you might not have heard of. It's called *How Insensitive.*'

Thierry grinned broadly.

'Ah? So, you do know it then?'

'Indeed! Yes, it was a minor hit here in the 1990s. I think it was a version by that Irish singer…erm…Sinéad O'Connor. It was a particular favourite of my wife.'

'Oh, well that's great!' Amy continued, 'Actually, Thierry, I searched high and low for French lyrics to it but I can't find them. So … I've taken the liberty of … writing my own.'

'Is it a direct translation of the English lyrics?'

Not really,' replied Amy.

'Oh!' said Thierry. 'And is it very different?'

Amy smiled. 'In a way. It's from the opposite point of view. I've changed the song in the French version to address the pain of a person who has lost someone … lost someone they loved.'

'Perhaps the loss of … a child?' asked Thierry.

Amy nodded. 'Perhaps.'

'May I see the new lyrics?' Thierry continued.

Amy passed over a sheet of paper and he carefully read her composition.

'Wow!' he said slowly. 'Those new lyrics are ... really something! Good Aimée. Good for you! So, what's the structure of the song going to be?'

'Not very complicated!' Amy laughed. 'I thought, first time through the original song in English, second time through my version in French.'

Thierry pondered this for a moment.

'How about an instrumental section in between?'

'That would be fabulous!' said Amy. She looked across at me and I shrugged. 'But we haven't prepared anything like that.'

'What key are you in?' Thierry asked.

Amy looked at me again.

'D minor,' I replied, delighted to be able to make some sort of musical contribution to the discussion.

Thierry smiled. 'Yes, that works for me ... if you would like me to, I could include something in between!'

'Mais oui!' we both said together.

He turned to me. 'Hey Pete, did you bring your guitar. I'd love to hear it.'

I went to the car and returned with my guitar.

We set ourselves up in the little studio and Amy arranged her lyrics on the music stand. I spotted Thierry quietly pressing the red 'record' button just before we began. As promised, we sang through both versions, first in English and then in French. Thierry sat with his chin resting on his hand — listening carefully.

'That was just fabulous, both of you!' he said when we finished. Actually, I've taken a sneaky recording so that I can prepare an instrumental part for tomorrow!'

We listened back and Amy seemed quite happy with what she'd done.

Then Amy asked, 'Thierry, do we have to record the whole song in one go or can we do each part separately?'

'Whatever you prefer, Aimée. Many of my artists prefer to make the recording in one go. Others like to split it into two or three separate parts. We can easily record the English verse and the French verse separately—just as long as you're happy to use headphones and, Pete, as long as you can use a click track through your cans—that way we can keep the same tempo throughout and join everything up seamlessly at the end.'

After Amy had translated to me exactly what Thierry had said, I replied 'Fine by me!'

Then Thierry added, 'I sometimes try to layer in percussion and a bass onto recordings but in this case, I'd prefer it stripped right down … just voice and guitar. It will be close-mic-ed so we can really hear the emotion in Amy's voice. It's going to be fantastic!'

Amy made a face. 'If you say so, Thierry! Oh, the pressure! But I'll do my best!'

One day plus two hours later we were almost done! Thierry had inserted a dreamy improvisation played on his piano keyboard which he subsequently re-voiced as an oboe. After some discussion we agreed to end the recording with a reprise of the oboe finale so I re-recorded a few more chords to accompany Thierry's final flourish.

Thierry treated us to a coffee and then produced a bag of Danish pastries. We settled into the little listening area to give our recording a final check. I had to admit that it all sounded wonderful and even my old guitar had acquired a majestic tone that I'd never heard from it before. Thierry's improvisations really did add a lot to the overall structure of the arrangement. But above everything else, what shone was Amy's voice. This was the first time that either of us had heard it properly recorded and it just sounded 'formidable'. Well done Thierry! Fantastic job!

'Is everyone happy?' Thierry asked.

We both grinned at him.

'What's French for ecstatic?' I asked Amy.

'Fou de joie, Thierry! We are really delighted!'

Then I asked 'Thierry, we haven't discussed money at all. Time is money for you and we must pay you!'

But Thierry would have none of it. 'No, no. I originally created my studio to give a voice to local people. You are certainly local, Aimée — born in … somewhere near here … and I'd love to help you in any way I can. Who knows? You may have started out on a journey to become the pride of Normandy!'

'But you have to make a living, Thierry,' Amy continued. 'Please!'

Thierry pondered for a moment and then grinned. 'OK then. This one is free — I insist on that. But when the music world comes knocking at your door and you want to record your first album … well perhaps you'd remember me!'

Amy promised that she would.

35

Two days later, at 8am, Amy and I were walking through the front door of the Radio Calvados studio in Lisieux. We were met by a very animated Marcel who seemed to have undergone something of a personality change since we had last met him just three weeks earlier. He explained that Amy was to be the initial subject of a new weekly series called "Where are they now?" Each episode was scheduled to last just twenty minutes and was designed to provide an update on a story previously covered by the station. Where possible, there should also be a musical connection, so clearly Amy ticked every box!

'In fact, yours was by far the most popular story of the year, Aimée,' Marcel continued, 'and people will be fascinated to hear if there have been any developments since your last broadcast.'

Amy made a face. 'I wish I had better news to report, Marcel, but at least I was able to talk briefly to my dad and he told me a bit more about my mother.'

Marcel grinned. 'That's brilliant!' he said. 'A step forward! We can go through those details before the interview.'

Marcel went on to explain that, unlike the first series, this broadcast would not be live so she could be very relaxed about stopping the recording at any point and revisiting what was being discussed.

'Well, that takes the pressure off! 'said a relieved Amy. 'So,' he continued, 'after your interview I'll be spending the rest of the morning editing the recordings. The final 20-minute programme will be broadcast at 2PM today.'

'Hmm, busy day for you, Marcel' I remarked.

'Actually, I'm really looking forward to it! I can't tell you!' he replied with a grin.

'Who's interviewing me, Marcel?' Amy asked.

He looked at the floor and briefly shuffled his feet.

'Well, guess what?' he replied. 'Your interviewer this time will be ... me!'

'Wow!' said Amy. 'Great! How did that happen?'

Marcel smiled modestly. 'Well, I was actually very inspired by your story ... how you overcame your shyness and just got out there and did it. So, I asked if I could do this one ... and they said yes. It's my first time, so ...'

'No worries, Marcel,' I beamed at him. 'Amy's now an expert with, erm, interviews so you can both be, what's the word, brilliant together! It will be twenty minutes of perfection!'

'Actually,' Marcel replied, 'when you include the two songs, it's just 15 minutes of chat. We'll start with "Où est Ma Mère?" and end with "How Insensitive". Oh, yes, Thierry sent me the new recording!'

'And did you like it, Marcel?' I asked.

He blushed slightly and suddenly was a bit lost for words. 'Well, no actually...I didn't... erm...just *like* it. I thought it was...it was...really quite magnificent! I *loved* it!'

I clapped him on the back. 'Well said, Marcel! Me too!'

He turned to address Amy. 'Aimée, I should like to say to you about your voice. It has great emotion. It feels like...well, you have such a talent, and I think...this could be the start of something really special!'

Now it was Amy's turn to blush.

Over the next 50 minutes, Marcel gave Amy a more detailed outline of what he had planned to ask her about. He also let Amy update him on developments since the first broadcast. This included a number of details about Élise that she had not known three weeks earlier; for example her age, where she had lived previously and the fact that she had a lovely singing voice. Amy also outlined our plans to visit newspaper offices, local government agencies, charities, music societies and much more, to see if anyone had a memory of

185

Élise and could indicate where she may have moved on to. Finally, Amy pointed out that she had been only three years old when she was taken away. She was now 23, so in a way this was a sort of weird 20th anniversary of this sad event.

An hour and a half later, as Amy and I drove home, I asked her how she felt it all had gone.

'Pretty good, I think,' she replied. 'I really wasn't nervous. Because it wasn't live, the pressure was nothing like last time. But also, I really wanted Marcel to shine so thinking about helping him to do well stopped me worrying about myself!'

'Well done you!' I responded. 'Can't wait to hear it this afternoon!'

Marcel made his 2PM editing deadline. We sat down to listen and the 20 minutes fairly flew by. I couldn't grasp everything but, as far as I could tell, the programme zipped along in a friendly and lively manner. Amy sounded very confident and there seemed to be real chemistry between her and her novice interviewer.

Fortunately, Amy was happy with the result and the second song was, naturally, a triumph. The final minute of the broadcast comprised Marcel including a most moving tribute to Amy. He praised the quality of her singing and he also put her "où est ma mère" campaign firmly back on track and into the listeners' consciousness. He ended with the question, "What Aimée has done was so very brave. How many of us would take such a risk for love?"

Bien joué, Marcel!

36

That evening at around 6PM we were settling into a celebratory glass of something alcoholic and a few nibbles. There was the sound of a car on the drive, shortly followed by a knock on the door. How unusual, we thought, as we *never* get visitors! It was Marcel. We welcomed him in like a returning hero from the Crusades, sat him down and thrust a glass into his hand.

'It was great, Marcel. Really great!' Amy began. 'Well done!'

'What did *you* think, Marcel?' I added.

He looked a little ill at ease.

'Well...,' he began.

Amy was concerned. 'Is anything wrong, Marcel?'

'No ... no, not really. I thought the programme was...well, very good. Excellent, in fact. And you were also great, Aimée!' He paused.

'But...?' Amy offered.

'Well, it's just that there has been a...development since the broadcast.'

We both set down our glasses.

'A development!' said Amy slowly. 'What sort of development?'

'Well,' said Marcel softly. 'I've been contacted...by a woman...'

'And...?' I said encouragingly.

'And...' he went on. 'And I think...she might be...your mother.'

Wow! He'd just come straight out with it!

Amy was unable to move. She tried to speak but no sound came out. We both stared at each other and then back at Marcel in shocked silence.

Eventually Marcel spoke. He took out his mobile and dialled. 'Aimée, would you like to speak to her?'

Tears began to form at the corners of her eyes. She nodded weakly. Then he put his phone on speaker and handed it to Amy.

'Hello, Aimée,' came a tearful female voice.

'Is it really you?'

'Yes, my darling, it is really me. This is your mother.'

Amy was unable to reply, so the disembodied voice continued.

'I know. Perhaps you must find it difficult to believe me…so… let me tell you. My name is Élise Camille Charpentier. I'm 43 years of age.'

Marcel quietly got out of his chair and opened the door.

Amy, still in a daze, continued the conversation.

'Yes, and … what happened 20 years ago?'

The door opened and into the room, still holding a mobile to her ear, came Amy's double, but just a little older. The visitor lowered her phone and continued the conversation directly.

'Twenty years ago,' she replied. 'Twenty years ago, Maurice took you from me. I waited and waited at Lisieux station but … he never returned.'

Amy lifted her head and turned it to the door. Their eyes met. Suddenly, they both dropped their phones on the floor and rushed towards each other. The sobbing embrace lasted a full minute.

Then Élise spoke once more. 'We have a lifetime of conversations ahead of us, but first I have something important to do.'

She nodded at Marcel who once again opened the door. Standing outside, hand in hand, were two teenagers, a girl of about 15 and a boy of 13.

'These are Charlotte and Fabien,' Élise said softly. 'Children, this is your sister, Aimée. Come and say hello!'

Screaming in unison they ran across the room and practically knocked Amy over in the excitement of this miraculous family reunion. All four collapsed onto the sofa, kissing, hugging and stroking each other's cheeks.

Suddenly, Amy stood up.

'I have also something important to say.'

She gestured towards me. 'This is my wonderful boyfriend, Pete.' She smiled at me. 'Please be kind to him—he's English!'

Then she said to me in English, 'Pete, this is my … this is my …' She shouted the final two words of the sentence, 'French family!'

At this point Amy let out a piercing scream which immediately set off the rest of her French family. I went over and gave them all a hug. My own greetings were a little more modest than anything Amy had been dishing out but still very heartfelt.

And now the conversations began in earnest and at a speed of Mach 20. Marcel quietly got up to depart but I pulled him back to his chair. 'You stay there, Marcel. I'm going to need an interpreter!' And so it continued — Amy's family talking frantically *vingt à la douzaine*, with Marcel trying his best to keep me in the loop with what was going on. It was hysterical!

He explained that Élise and family lived just outside Paris. She was now married with a partner called Henri. They had all recently spent two weeks on a camping holiday in Northern Spain, which was why she missed news of the first broadcast. She had a sister who lived in Caen and it was she who alerted her to the upcoming broadcast that was transmitted this afternoon. After listening to the first few minutes online, she had immediately rounded up the kids and they all jumped on a train to Lisieux.

Marcel listened silently for a few more minutes as the family's mood began to change. Their conversation became noticeably calmer and quiet and I could see that all four of them were looking upset. I looked over at Marcel and discovered that he was welling up also. I gave his sleeve a firm tug and said, 'Marcel, please, what's going on now?'

After spending a few moments composing himself, he explained that, when Aimée was taken, Élise correctly surmised that Maurice would have brought her to England. But with no money and without a passport, she had no idea how to set about finding her. Eventually, with the help of her sister, she was able to make her way to London. Her first stop was with the French embassy. They were very helpful and contacted the British police but the police were useless. Élise doesn't think they tried very hard to find them. She felt they saw it just as a domestic dispute and since Amy was with her father there was nothing they could do. Her money ran out, so she had to come home. She came over again the following year but still no luck. She tried social media but nothing ever came of her efforts. Nothing … until now!

After about 15 minutes, there was a brief pause in the conversational mayhem that had taken over the Charpentier family. At this point, quite unexpectedly, Charlotte and Fabien stood up and walked over to where Marcel and I were sitting. In thoughtful consideration of her sister's English boyfriend, Charlotte started speaking very slowly to us both. She said that Marcel had told them in the car about Amy's song and they still hadn't had the chance to hear it. She wondered if perhaps he had brought a recording with him for them to hear. She spoke so clearly that even I could understand her request. Marcel sadly shook his head but then I interjected, 'I think we can do better than that, Charlotte.' I picked up my guitar from the stand.

I called across to Amy, 'Hey Amy, we've had a request. Do you think you could manage your first live public performance?' Her eyes widened, registering a slight shock at being suddenly put on the spot. 'Um…' was all she was able to say.

'I'm taking that as a "Yes", then,' I smiled back at her.

Amy nodded 'OK.' She waved Charlotte and Fabien back to where they had been sitting and opened her laptop to display the French lyrics that she had composed. She placed it on Élise's lap for her mother and her siblings to see and began to sing in French while I strummed.

How sensitive
I've become
When I learned your heart got broken
How distressed and sad
You must have been
On the day he took me from you

Long, long years have passed
I know at last we'll be reunited
Just to hold your hand
Give me your hand
And our sadness will be ended.

It was a moving moment and everyone just sat quietly thinking about the poignancy of the words at this particular time and in this setting. Élise took Amy's hand in hers and once again kissed it.

The silence was broken by a tearful Élise. 'I know this song. Sinéad erm, Sinéad O'Connor! I used to sing it!'

Amy looked across at me and nodded, 'Play it again, Pete!'

I played the chords once more and everyone present shared a moment of happy intimacy as the two soulful voices joined as one. Then Élise whispered, '*Enfin chez nous, ma petite poulette*'— home at last my little chicken.

July 2025

If I were a gambling man, I'd have put money on it that none of this would have happened. What are the chances of finding one woman in a population of 68 million people? But, however long it took, I knew she'd never have given up.

Amy talks with her mum all the time—well at least twice a week. We get over there to see them when we can, even if it's only for the occasional weekend. But to be honest, I've been hampered by my limited mastery of the language so I was finally pushed into doing something about it. Amy found a French conversation class with a teacher who has the wonderful name of Fanny La Belle. We meet in the local café—just me and three other women of a certain age. Sometimes it feels a bit like a Women's Institute meeting but it's good fun and actually I feel flattered that they include me on the team as an honorary doyenne. My French has definitely got better over the past year, but the real winner is my blossoming insight into the world of arts & crafts, moisturising cream, and the joys of hormone replacement therapy!

When I look back at my life before I met Amy, it's hard to believe how much has changed. And not just for me but for the whole family. Annie's over the moon. It didn't surprise me that she organised a pre-Christmas party for twelve in Slieve Gallion—both UK and French sides. It was a great do and I was so pleased that mum and dad managed to be there. We all contributed to the food— I'm not sure what it was that Élise had made but there was more lemon and garlic in it than I'd ever eaten in my life. Plans are afoot this summer to repeat the event and Harry and Sam look forward to dragging their French visitors into a bit of regatta magic on the Orbiquet river.

Amy rang Marta the minute we got back home. She and Annette immediately invited themselves round clutching a bottle of champagne to share in the celebration. And now, it was all 'our lovely girl' this and 'our lovely girl' that. Where was 'my lovely boy'? I never got a look in! Amy also wanted to tell her dad. I let her do that one on her own. I expect he wasn't too thrilled to want to celebrate her good news. She pops round to see him occasionally and I suspect she slips him the occasional few quid.

When Amy got back to work and I had three months left to tackle my thesis in the calm and quiet of the flat, I finally got it finished. And though I do say so myself, it isn't half bad. I stuck to my original title "What are the Chances of that Happening?" partly because, well, it's about chance and probability, but also because it reminds me of my initial doubts as to whether Amy would ever actually find her mother! How wrong was I about that one? Anyway, as of this week I'm officially signing autographs as Doctor Peter Campbell.

Are mum and dad thrilled about that? You bet they are! They even sent me a birthday card with Doctor Peter Campbell on the envelope.

When the news of my doctorate came through, Stacey organised a drink-up for me in her office. Her husband and two kids turned up as well, which was very touching. All the secretaries pitched in with putting up decorations and making me little presents. Blimey—I don't mind telling you I was fighting back tears when all that was going on! There'll be a faculty 'do' next week as well but it'll be this little informal event organised by Stacey, Amy and the others that will really stay in my memory for a long time.

The lunch date Clare threatened never happened—I knew it wouldn't. I do feel bad about the way I treated her that day she turned up at the flat. But there was so much else going on at the time…I couldn't handle it. She's probably gone back to America. We had always been two very different people who had gradually grown apart with each passing year. I just hope she's happy. Two people who definitely *are* happy are mum and dad. They were thrilled to hear that Amy had managed to find her mother but I suspect even more thrilled that their thirty seven year old son seems to have finally settled down. I know what would complete their joy. And yes, I will probably ask Amy sometime—I'm not getting any younger after all. But I know what will happen—I'll wake up one morning and it will all be arranged.

THE END